CHAPTER 1

INTRODUCTION

Never explain-your friends do not need it and your enemies will not believe you anyway.[1]

— Elbert Hubbard

We do not see things as they are; we see things as we are.[2]

— Anais Nin

Policy, Strategy, and Narratives

In 1992, President George H. W. Bush described the United States mission in Somalia as a humanitarian relief effort under the name Provide Relief.[3] That mission eventually transitioned to security and stability under Restore Hope.[4] By the summer of 1993, President William J. Clinton had inherited this mission and the American public had a sense of mission accomplishment.[5] In October of that year, a devastating shoot-down of a U.S. helicopter and the ensuing Battle of Mogadishu changed the dynamic. Six months later, the U.S. withdrew from Somalia altogether without ever reaching an agreement between the warring factions. Did the humanitarian and security requirements go away? Was the burden of the 18 U.S. servicemen killed that day enough to change our policy of U.S. support to Somalia? Or did the narrative about our involvement in Somalia change? In 2001, President George W. Bush described the U.S. policy towards al Qa'ida as a War on Terror,[6] that phrase has since been changed by President Barack Obama's administration to Overseas Contingency Operations.[7] Neither description accurately describes the national policy that attempts to disrupt terrorist networks and secure U.S.

1

interests, but did our policy towards al-Qa'ida and other terrorist organizations change?

Or did it just get a new description, in essence a new narrative?

It has been said that the United States withdrew militarily from Iraq in 2011 because the two governments were unable to reach a Status of Forces Agreement amenable to both parties,[8] yet less than three years later the U.S. military was back in Iraq without a change to the existing agreement. Did our policy change with respect to a post-war support agreement? Did the need to protect our military members with a valid Status of Forces Agreement change? Or is it possible, that our understanding of the situation changed and thus the narrative supporting the policy changed? These are just a few examples of the complex relationship between our understanding of a problem, our narrative of that understanding, and the policy efforts attempting to achieve our national interests. Determining the relationship between narratives and their corresponding policies is difficult, but one way to make sense of complex relationships is to deconstruct and analyze the individual parts. By looking at policy, strategy, and narrative independently, we can then reconstruct a possible framework for understanding their intricate relationship.

In their book, *Ideas as Weapons: Influence and Perception in Modern Warfare*, editors David and McKeldin identify four broad categories of perspectives; Geopolitical, Strategic, Operational, and Tactical; where "the Geopolitical is dominated by world politics, diplomacy, and the elements of national power other than military force."[9] This is further complicated by the views of the insurgents themselves. As Col Thomas Hammes points out in his article, *Information Warfare*, "in the information arena, the tactical, operational, and strategic levels of war merge."[10] However, one premise for understanding policy, according to Harry Yarger, Professor of National Security Policy at the U.S. Army War College, is that policy is "the clear articulation of guidance for the employment of the instruments of power towards the attainment of one or more objectives or end states."[11] In simpler terms, a policy can be seen as a principle or statement of intent to guide decisions and achieve national objectives.

As compared to law or regulation, policy merely guides decision-making and does not compel or prohibit behavior. Regardless of the heuristic or approach used to understand the cycle of policy, it almost always starts with identification of the problem or issue. This step is important, in that our understanding of the problem or issue is potentially biased by our cultural values, attitudes, and beliefs. This understanding contributes to how we describe the problem or issue and what course of action can best achieve our desired end states. But describing the problem and the desired end states is not enough. We must also have a way to achieve those end states and the means to support those efforts. Many times, an end state can be achieved incrementally by achieving certain ends. In the military, this is understood as ends, ways, and means. If policy describes the end states, then what describes the ends, ways, and means? Some theorists suggest a way to describe this collection of ends, ways, and means, is as strategy. If Yarger's assertion that policy guides employment of power, then it follows that policy must naturally dominate strategy in that it articulates the desired end state and guides the use of resources, considerations, limitations, or even actions. Even with this simplistic understanding of policy and strategy, one is still left wondering how a narrative of that policy or strategy supports, enhances, or clarifies the policy or strategy in question. In the most mundane sense, which comes first, the narrative or the policy? Or is it possible that the relationship between narratives and policies is more complicated than merely what comes first?

How we describe problems and issues may give insight to our understanding of those problems and, quite possibly, into our underlying cultural values, attitudes, and beliefs. The language and context in those descriptions can be described as a narrative. Defining narratives is, like many abstract concepts, problematic. In the most basic sense, "narratives are a way of structuring and communicating our understanding of the world."[12] Another definition of narratives suggests, "A narrative is a story constructed to give meaning to things and events."[13] Central to these definitions is that constituents, whether they are individuals, groups, or countries, have narratives, which reflect and reveal how they define themselves and their surroundings.[14] Both of these definitions support the idea that a narrative is influenced by one's understanding of themselves and their environment. So does the narrative communicate our understanding of the problem or does it legitimize the policy end state? Does it describe the strategic ends, ways, and means or justify the accompanying strategy?

If there is a hierarchy to policy and strategy, is there then a hierarchy of narratives? Yarger suggests a strategy hierarchy that flows from National Interests to a Grand Strategy, to National Policies, to the National Security Strategy, to the instrument of power specific Strategy, which then continues to the Theater, Operational, and Tactical level strategies, what he terms the Comprehensiveness of Strategy.

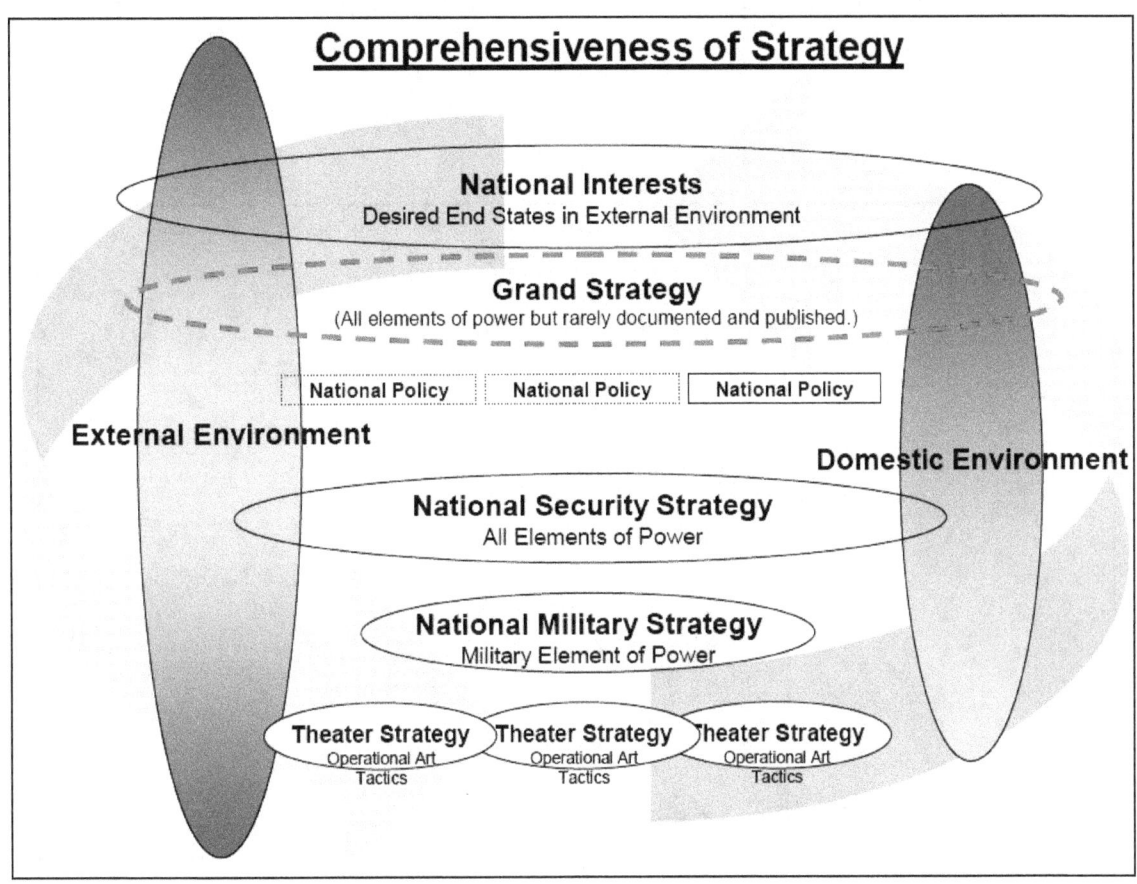

Figure 1.   Comprehensiveness of Strategy

Source: Harry R. Yarger, "Strategic Theory for the 21st Century: The Little Book on Big Strategy" (Monograph, Strategic Studies Institute, U.S. Army War College, February 2006), 9, accessed October 7, 2014, http://www.strategicstudiesinstitute.army.mil/pubs/download.cfm?q=641.

With the assumption that this is a generally accepted framework, even if one considers the depiction an unnecessarily static and confined representation, it follows then that there is likely a hierarchy of narratives as well. There could be a meta-narrative that is a collective understanding of the world both as it is and how we wish it to be, followed by a narrative supporting the policy, which in turn is supported by narratives among the various levels of strategic discourse. A graphical depiction could be viewed as the following.

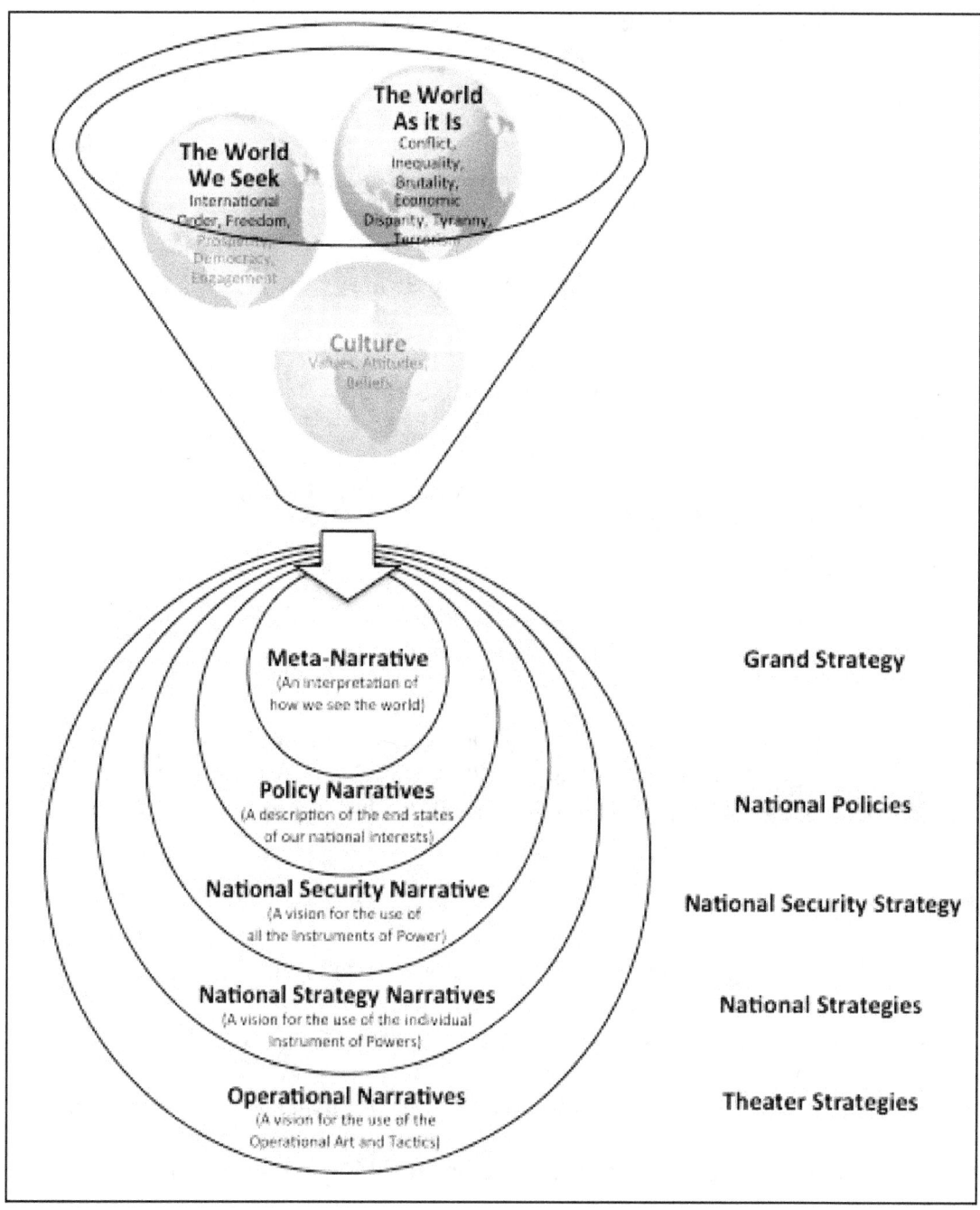

Figure 2. Graphic Representation of Policy, Strategy, and Narratives

Source: Created by author.

While this representation may be overly simplistic, it provides an understanding for determining potential relationships between narratives and policy. In this respect, the narrative not only helps to communicate to the intended audiences but also serves to inform decision makers of the problems they are facing. By making sense of what one sees, identifying where the story begins and ends, and trying to describe what happened and why, policymakers can begin to shape their policy efforts. In this regard, one can define policy narratives as those descriptions of the environment, situation, actors, and problems, which are used for policymaking regarding a specific issue due to its complexity, uncertainty, or polarization. Finally, narratives, policy, strategic, or otherwise, are simplifications that help decision makers make sense of complex problems that could otherwise induce policy or strategy paralysis. As described by Mike Shanahan, narratives "generate consensus around major policies and make political action possible."[15]

Many casual readers of information practices and the use of a narrative may wonder as to the importance of a narrative. Recent events across the globe both from foreign governments, such as Russia's involvement in the Ukraine, and from violent extremist organizations, such as the Islamic State's recent beheadings, prove that messaging and narratives are important. Additionally, narratives serve as vehicles of influence. This aspect of influence is important as well, in that influence is a central part of diplomacy, often seen as "the heart of diplomacy."[16] Narratives provide a powerful tool for that influence. One could propose that the importance of the narrative has followed the information age and expansion of the Internet and new media, but history proves otherwise. This was evidenced during the complicated foreign policy years of nuclear deterrence throughout the Cold War. So much so that the "U.S. Advisory Commission on Public Diplomacy reported . . . [we must] improve the accuracy and political impact of words and terms used by our leaders in speaking to the world."[17]

It is not enough to have a narrative that suits policy goals; it must also resonate with the target audience. Howard Gardner, cognitive scientist and professor at Harvard's Graduate School of Education, suggests that "the story must be simple, easy to identify with, emotionally resonant, and evocative of positive experiences."[18] He continues to suggest that messages resonate best with homogenous groups, however that certainly is not the case when the target audience is the whole world, as J. Michael Waller suggests in his book, *Fighting the War of Ideas Like a Real War*. Using synchronized themes, messages, actions, and images can be critical to shaping conditions for effective advancement of U.S. policy objectives. The manner people receive and interpret information is influenced by their ideology, ethnocentricity, and culture. Even with a framework for understanding policy and strategy, a potential understanding that there are multiple narratives among varying levels of discourse, and that narratives are ways we communicate our understanding, one still wonders as to the true relationship between narratives and policy, especially when they seem disparate or in direct conflict.

The Importance of Narratives in the U.S. Policy

To understand the relationship of narratives in U.S. policymaking, one must first develop an understanding of why narratives are important. U.S. Army Field Manual 3-24.2, *Tactics in Counterinsurgency*, describes a narrative as a way for "interpreting other's intentions" and thus defines the narrative as a "central mechanism through which ideologies are expressed."[19] As mentioned earlier, understanding the narrative is complicated by the many voices competing to get their messages heard. In this multitude of narratives, it can be difficult to define who offers the U.S. policy narrative, but for the purposes of this study, the author assumes these will originate from office of the President, the Department of State, and official representatives of the legislative and executive branches. To help define who offers the preponderance of the narrative, one can once again turn to Waller, in his book *Fighting the War of Ideas Like a Real War*, who proposes that the U.S. Department of State (DOS) dominates the U.S. governments (USG's) global message content.[20] He suggests that the DOS has three main elements in its narrative construction, first "offer a positive vision of hope and opportunity," second, "isolate and marginalize the violent extremists," and lastly, "foster a sense of common interests and common values."[21] Therefor he suggests the audience for this U.S. policy discourse is the whole world.[22] If narratives tell the story of the problem, the actors, a potential solution, accompany each level of policy and strategy, and are competing for legitimation among the policymakers, then how are narratives produced and what is their relationship with policy?

The Purpose of This Study

This thesis attempts to understand the relationship between policy narratives and their corresponding policy efforts. Is there a straightforward answer to which comes first, the policy or the narrative? Or is the relationship much more complicated than that? Do pre-existing narratives influence policy decisions or do changes in policy require new narratives for policy legitimation? Is there a dominant element between a policy and the narrative? While these are equally intriguing questions, the relationship between narratives and policy is certainly complex. Additionally, this study will hopefully confirm existing theories of narrative policy relationships or identify areas for future research. Finally, this work hopes to communicate how understanding this relationship can help policymakers, senior decision makers, interagency partners, and battlefield commanders.

Thesis Question

The primary research question driving this study is: What is the relationship between a policy and the accompanying narrative? There are several supporting questions, which seek to address the primary question; (1) does a narrative precede the policy, or does the policy precede the narrative? (2) To what extent or in what manor do pre-existing narratives influence policy decisions when the policy problem changes, (3) does a change in policy mean a change in the policy narrative or meta-narrative, (4) do narratives legitimize policy decisions, (5) can successful narrative and policy change analysis occur over periods of less than ten years, (6) can narratives contribute to instability, and finally, (7) how can the choice of a particular narrative result in missed opportunities? These research questions help shape the subject area of interest and provide insight into potential shifts in narrative and policy. Furthermore, the multitude of narratives, from a variety of sources, often creates a din in the media. This is especially true for those who argue, "We are still fighting more to get the message out than waging a full-blown influence war against our enemies."[23] By focusing on the U.S. policy narrative the author hopes to provide clarity to the development of situational understanding vis-à-vis official USG policy and diplomacy. Unfortunately, this narrowly scoped definition of who provides the U.S. policy narrative is also a limitation of the research.

Assumptions

The facts used to support the research include official statements offered by representatives of the USG; credible statements attributed to those individuals whether or not they are official statements, and published strategy documents such as the National Security Strategy (NSS), and other official U.S. policy and doctrine. Finally, the author assumes that official statements are an insight to the narrative at work in a given policy and that public opinion as represented by credible polling sources might serve as an indicator of the success or failure of that narrative.

Limitations

Unfortunately, this paper is limited to the policy narrative based upon readily available and unclassified information and therefore, does not contain any classified activities employed by the various agencies seeking to support a particular policy. Additionally, aside from very brief experience as an all-source intelligence analyst in the mid-1990s, the author has very limited experience with discourse analysis, social psychology, foreign policy, or public diplomacy. As previously mentioned, there are not readily available instruments that measure how effective a particular narrative is or is not, therefore these influences are inferred based on the results of various polling agencies throughout the selected research time period. Finally, the author is an active duty service member in the United States Air Force and, as such, may present a bias for or against a particular course of action based on prior military experience in special operations, however, every effort will be made to prevent the author's bias from influencing the research in this study.

Delimitations

This paper will narrow the focus and research to policy narratives and policy. As such, the considerations for strategic, operational, or tactical narratives are not reviewed. Additionally, the case study reviewed, the U.S. Syrian narrative, only encompasses that which is developed by the administration at the time of the civil war. This limited review is intended to aid in understanding a single and consistent official policy narrative from one administration. It is possible that previous administrations may have distinctly different narratives of the same or similar circumstances.

Significance of the Study

This research represents an entrepreneurial effort into understanding the nodal linkages between narratives with various themes and messages and the policy and strategy employed by the USG. Additionally, this research presents considerations for influence and diplomacy beyond the range of military operations in a whole of society approach to complex problem solving. Finally, it is important to note that the use of information as an instrument of national power is a "powerful tool to influence, disrupt, corrupt, or usurp an adversary's ability to make and share decisions."[24] This study may be applicable to all levels of discourse, not just those centered on the policy debate. If policy informs strategy, and narratives accompany both, the results of this study could inform decision makers at all levels across the many disciplines.

The next chapter will review the literature on this topic and provide an assessment of the significance of that material to this study. It will be followed by an explanation of the methodology and then subsequent chapters examining the issue in detail followed by the author's personal assessment and conclusions.

Definition of Terms

Message: Any thought or idea expressed briefly in a language and prepared in a form suitable for transmission by any means of communication. Often times, a message is a narrowly focused communication directed at a specific audience to support a specific theme.[25]

Narrative: A story constructed to give meaning to things and events.[26]

National Policy: A broad course of action adopted by a federal government in pursuit of its objectives.[27] Shortened in this thesis as policy, or USG policy.

Policy Narrative: Those narratives, descriptions of the environment, situation, actors, and problems, that are used by a political entity for policymaking regarding a specific issue due to its complexity, uncertainty, or polarization.

Propaganda: Any form of adversary communication, especially of a biased or misleading nature, designed to influence the opinions, emotions, attitudes, or behavior of any group in order to benefit the sponsor, either directly or indirectly.[28]

Public Affairs: Those public information, command information, and community engagement activities directed toward both the external and internal publics with interest in the Department of Defense.[29]

Public Diplomacy: Those overt international public information activities of the United States Government designed to promote United States foreign policy objectives by seeking to understand, inform, and influence foreign audiences and opinion makers, and by broadening the dialogue between American citizens and institutions and their counterparts abroad. In peace building, civilian agency efforts to promote an understanding of the reconstruction efforts, rule of law, and civic responsibility through public affairs and international public diplomacy operations.[30]

Strategic Communications: Focused USG efforts to understand and engage key audiences to create, strengthen, or preserve conditions favorable for the advancement of United States Government interests, policies, and objectives through the use of coordinated programs, plans, themes, messages, and products synchronized with the actions of all instruments of national power.[31] For the military, SC can be further subdivided into Public Affairs and Information Operations.

---

[1] Elbert Hubbard, *The Motto Book* (East Aurora, NY: Roycroft Press, 1907). Hubbard founded the Roycroft effort in East Aurora, New York, and became a prolific writer after his inspiration pamphlet, *A Message to Garcia*. In an anthology of mottos, he includes this truism. It is incredibly germane to the battle of the narratives. If it holds true, then the battle is already lost. Hopefully this study will provide clarity to Hubbard's statement.

[2] Anais Nin, *Seduction of the Minotaur* (Chicago, IL: Swallow Press, 1961). In this autobiographical novel Nin follows the story and psychoanalysis of a woman named Lillian. It is likely that Nin was capitalizing on the Freudian concept of the "monster" subconscious that must be seduced instead of killed in order to deal with the underlying issues. Although this reference is often disputed, as Nin attributes it to an old Talmudic saying, it speaks to a universal understanding that we see the world through our own lens. This concept is critically important in understanding the battle of narratives.

[3] George H. W. Bush, *Address to the Nation on the Situation in Somalia*, The American Presidency Project, December 4, 1992, accessed October 31, 2014, http://www.presidency.ucsb.edu/ws/?pid=21758. In this address to the nation, President G. H. W. Bush describes the U.S. mission in Somalia as the following: "For many

months now, the United States has been actively engaged in the massive international relief effort to ease Somalia's suffering."

[4] Ibid. In December of 1992, President G. W. H. Bush outlined his plan for increasing security in Somalia.

[5] William J. Clinton, *Letter to Congressional Leaders on the Situation in Somalia*, The American Presidency Project, June 10, 1993, accessed October 31, 2014, http://www.presidency.ucsb.edu/ws/?pid=46676. In this letter to Congress, President Clinton describes the results of Operation Restore Hope as successful.

[6] George W. Bush, *Address Before a Joint Session of the Congress on the United States Response to the Terrorist Attacks of September 11*, The American Presidency Project, September 20, 2001, accessed October 31, 2014, http://www.presidency.ucsb. edu/ws/?pid=64731. President Bush first used the expression War on Terror before a Joint Session of the Congress.

[7] Oliver Burkeman, "Obama Administration Says Goodbye to 'War on Terror'," *The Guardian*, March 25, 2009, accessed November 2, 2014, http://www.theguardian. com/world/2009/mar/25/obama-war-terror-overseas-contingency-operations. In this article by *The Guardian*, Burkeman describes the name change as originating in "A message sent recently to senior Pentagon staff explains that "this administration prefers to avoid using the term Long War or Global War On Terror (GWOT)."

[8] Lara Jakes and Rebecca Santana, "Iraq Withdrawal: U.S. Abandoning Plans To Keep Troops in Country," *The Huffington Post*, October 25, 2011, accessed November 2, 2014, http://www.huffingtonpost.com/2011/10/15/iraq-withdrawal-us-troops_n_ 1012661.html.

[9] G. J. David, Jr. and T. R. McKeldin III, eds., *Ideas as Weapons: Influence and Perception in Modern Warfare* (Dulles, VA: Potomac Books, 2009), 4.

[10] Ibid., 27.

[11] Harry R. Yarger, "Strategic Theory for the 21st Century: The Little Book on Big Strategy" (Monograph, Strategic Studies Institute, February 2006), 10, accessed October 7, 2014, http://www.strategicstudiesinstitute.army.mil/pubs/ download.cfm?q=641.

[12] Elizabeth A. Shanahan, Michael D. Jones, and Mark K. McBeth, "Policy Narratives and Policy Processes," *Policy Studies Journal* 39, no. 3 (2011): 539.

[13] U.S. Department of the Army, Army Doctrine Publication 5-0, *The Operations Process* (Washington, DC: U.S. Department of the Army, May 2012), 2-27.

[14] Ibid.

[15] Mike Shanahan, "What's in a narrative? In Policy, Everything or Nothing," *International Institute for Environment and Development*, September 28, 2012, accessed September 17, 2014, http://www.iied.org/what-s-narrative-policy-everything-or-nothing.

[16] U.S. Joint Chiefs of Staff, Joint Publication 3-13, *Information Operations* (Washington, DC: U.S. Joint Chiefs of Staff, November, 2012), II-1.

[17] J. Michael Waller, *Fighting the War of Ideas Like a Real War* (Washington, DC: The Institute of World Politics, 2007), 45.

[18] Alan Deutschman, "Change or Die," Fast Company, May 2005, accessed August 11, 2014, http://www.fastcompany.com/52717/change-or-die. Howard Gardner, a cognitive scientist, MacArthur Fellow "genius" award winner, and professor at Harvard's Graduate School of Education, has looked at what works most effectively for heads of state and corporate CEOs. "When one is addressing a diverse or heterogeneous audience," he says, "the story must be simple, easy to identify with, emotionally resonant, and evocative of positive experiences."

[19] U.S. Department of the Army, Field Manual 3-24.2, *Tactics in Counterinsurgency* (Washington, DC: U.S. Department of the Army, April 2009).

[20] Waller, *Fighting the War of Ideas*, 16.

[21] Ibid.

[22] Ibid., 20. "Our audience, therefore, is most of the entire world."

[23] Ibid., 19.

[24] U.S. Joint Chiefs of Staff, *Information Operations*, I-1.

[25] U.S. Joint Chiefs of Staff, Joint Publication 1-02, *Department of Defense Dictionary of Military and Associated Terms* (Washington, DC: U.S. Joint Chiefs of Staff, November 2010), 165.

[26] U.S. Department of the Army, *The Operations Process*, 2-27.

[27] Dictionary.com, "National Policy," accessed July 1, 2014, http://dictionary.reference.com/browse/ national+policy.

[28] U.S. Joint Chiefs of Staff, *Dictionary of Military and Associated Terms,* 207.

[29] Ibid., 208.

[30] Ibid.

[31] Ibid., 241.

CHAPTER 2

LITERATURE REVIEW

We debate the perfect without regard to the details . . . but the devil is in the details.[1]

— Matt Armstrong

Introduction

The literature on narratives, with its underlying themes and messages, as well as the analysis and design of policy is extensive, yet very little is written on the relationship between the two. This study will delve into the myriad of definitions, current meanings and provide context and background for the remainder of the paper. Additionally, this study will look at the social psychology aspect of narratives and attempt to reconcile the many definitions across the disciplines for the purposes of understanding the importance of a narrative and its implications for future policy making. This chapter will develop an understanding of policy, policy images, policy change as described in the Punctuated Equilibrium Theory, the Collective Action Framework, policy narratives, the Narrative Policy Framework as it applies to the meso-level Advocacy Coalition Framework, war narratives and war policy legitimization, and finally, attempt to reconcile the relationship between policy narratives and policymaking.

Policy Images and Punctuated-Equilibrium Theory

Perhaps one of the most cited works on policy and the supporting ideas that lead to policy change can be found in Punctuated-Equilibrium Theory[2] shortened in this study as PE Theory. PE theory is an evolutionary biology theory, which hypothesizes that for the majority of a geological history, a biological organism is in an extended state of equilibrium, or stasis. Significant change only comes with rare and rapid events that create branches of the species. The contrast to this theory is gradualism, where a species gradually changes over an extended period of time such that the descendants of the species can exhibit vastly different traits.

While this may not seem intuitive to policy and policy change, True, Jones, and Baumgartner in their seminal work of policy analysis, *Punctuated-Equilibrium Theory: Explaining Stability and Change in Public Policymaking*, suggest the same steady state exists in policy areas and is only rarely punctuated with significant change as crisis occurs.[3] According to the authors, one critical aspect of PE Theory is the concept of policy images. They suggest, "Policy images play a critical role in expanding issues beyond the control of the specialists and special interests."[4] They assert that the image is "generally connected to core political values and can be communicated simply and directly to the public."[5] This policy image is central to PE Theory in that when the fundamental understanding of the problem and the supporting policy image change dramatically, so to do the external pressures from additional policy actors and institutions. In this sense, if there is a disparity in the understanding or description of a particular policy among those who can change the policy, the contesting parties may each latch on to a particular image or sets of images that support their understanding of the policy.

For instance, the debate on immigration may serve as an example where differing sides may each visualize a set of images to enhance their argument for the policy. In this example, one side may describe the problem as Emma Lazarus' tired, poor, huddled masses yearning to breathe free, while another may describe it as a fiscal burden on the American taxpayers. In either case, the underlying images support the particular policy decision advocated and represent competing policy images and potential drivers of policy change.

True, Jones, and Baumgartner argue that when an agreed-upon image becomes contested, the policy in question is likely to be launched into the high agenda.[6] They also describe the importance of institutions, which they term venues, such as Congress, as they too can support or block policy change despite a change in policy image. Additionally, they suggest a reciprocal and iterative relationship where the pieces of the system can feed back into the whole as well.[7] Finally, they argue that policy images are a mechanism in the policy system from which policy decisions can be made and acted upon. In this sense, policy images could serve not only to inform a particular policy, but also to legitimate or otherwise justify that policy. Unfortunately, this understanding is not enough to describe the relationship between policy images and policy.

Images in International Relations

In addition to True, Jones, and Baumgartner, other scholars have studied the role of images in policymaking. Herrmann, Voss, Schooler, and Ciarrochi in their article, *Images in International Relations: An Experimental Test of Cognitive Schemata*, developed another theory for the study of images in international relations.[8] Herrmann, et al., suggest that regardless of the decision making model used to analyze the various types of reasoning, the foundation for the foreign policymaker's decision is their "construction of reality."[9] Herrmann et al., argue that this construction of reality, or in simpler terms, one's understanding of the situation, can be described as an image which then can be analyzed in the foreign policy domain. This image is described as a "cognitive, affective, and evaluative structure." However, to be useful in foreign policy analysis, this definition must be more clearly defined.[10] They offer three basic judgments used in decision making, which include: (1) the perceived relative capability of the opponent, (2) the perceived threat and/or opportunity, and (3) the perceived culture of the opponent.[11] Notice in all of these, it is the perception of the situation or opponent that guides the decision-making. Without explicitly describing it is as thus, the decision maker's perception speaks to the importance of their understanding of the situation or opponent, which is often influenced by the decision maker's own cultural values, attitudes, and beliefs. However, it is surprising that the author's did not include the perceived support for the policy by the policymaker's constituents. It is likely then that some of this calculus occurs during the perception of relative power.

This perception of relative power is, in fact, the basis of realist theory.[12] In this model, the strategic choices facing the decision maker are not only influenced by their estimate of the situation or opponent, but also a judgment of their own interests. If the perceived threats and opportunities drive policy change, it is the decision maker's assessment of relative power that determines the options available. In their analysis, the authors suggest that images are a causal variable in policy formation, but could not determine the relationship between affect and cognition. They did, however, discover that the imagery and policy choice are linked to affective and emotional components that might serve as an indicator of self-interest.[13]

Collective Action Framing

In attempting to understand the linkage between images and narratives, one possible construct is the Collective Action Frame (CAF). According to Benford and Snow's article, *Framing Processes and Social Movements: An Overview and Assessment*, collective action framing is an active process in which social movements derive understanding, or interpretive frames, that differ from existing ones and potentially challenge existing ways of understanding a problem or situation.[14] These collective action frames are more than just a way to simplify the collective understanding of the environment; they motivate action, generate support, and deter potential opponents.[15] In this respect collective action frames are "action-oriented sets of beliefs and meanings that inspire and legitimate the activities and campaigns."[16] In contrast to policy images, or other cognitive images for that matter, collective action frames are more than the aggregation of attitudes and perceptions; they also include the resulting shared understanding.[17] According to Benford and Snow, collective action frames have two distinct features; they are action-oriented and are supported with interactive, discursive processes.[18] This theory would suggest that collective action frames are the combination of policy images and a supporting policy narrative. The authors continue to suggest that collective action framing achieves both consensus mobilization and action mobilization, or in other words, "moving people from the balcony to the barricades."[19] This last component is especially important in driving policy change. Benford and Snow describe four basic justifications, which include severity, urgency, efficacy, and propriety.[20] It is important to note that the relative effectiveness of these motivations for action depend on how they are used in conjunction with each other and how they are received by their intended audience. They point out that in some instances the efficacy of the narrative can be diminished by an exaggerated severity or urgency.[21] They continue to suggest the greater the narrative's resonance with its intended audience, the more likely it will be accepted, and the more likely it will be acted upon.[22] Finally, a core component of CAF theory is the idea of a master frame, one that is wider in scope and influence than social movement frames. For example, a social movement for women's rights might draw on the master frame of equal rights for everyone. This relationship between a master frame and more narrowly focused social movement frames could serve as a justification for the hierarchy of narratives described earlier. In this sense, a policy narrative would use policy images found in a broader meta-narrative.

From this understanding of framing and collective action frames, it is easy to see that the discursive component of collective action framing is consistent with this study's definition of policy narrative. Benford and Snow point out that in some cases when the situation or environment has changed and in turn affected the frames resonance with its intended audience, it was then reframed.[23] If the assumption that a CAF encapsulates both the policy image and policy narrative is correct, then it is possible to suggest that when the environment changes, the policy narrative will change as well. What is not clear is if the underlying policy images change or just shift in priority. Regardless, the authors' theory of collective action framing does support the hypothesis that changes in policy images and policy narratives occur before a respective change in policy. The ambiguity in policy and political opportunities suggests that those problems are open to a variety of frames and, as such, a variety of narratives from a variety of voices.

Framing and Discourse

Although Benford and Snow's collective action framing emphasizes the discourse component, the actual impact of that discourse is only briefly explored. Marc Steinberg's article, *Tilting the Frame: Considerations on Collective Action Framing from a Discursive Turn*, offers a cogent argument for discourse exploration. Here, Steinberg builds on CAF theory by highlighting its deficiencies, but argues that the Bakhtin Circle[24] and social psychology can "provide some useful conceptual resolutions."[25] Steinberg offers five central areas that are unresolved in frame analysis. The first area of contention with Benford and Snow's argument is the relationship of ideology to the framing process. Left unresolved, according to Steinberg, is whether the frame is based on existing ideology, or if the ideology is an emergent product of the process?[26] Steinberg describes another critique of CAF theory in his desire to understand the manifestation of the frame, or in other words, how a frame is derived. In addition to these two critiques, Steinberg also raises the question of individual-collective linkages in the framing process, the difficulty of maintaining fidelity and alignment, and finally the relationship between discourse and material resources. He offers the conclusion that the ambiguities in alignment, centrality, credibility, and narrative fidelity raise questions as to whether the frame is an emergent practice of individual cognition or the combination and synchronization of meso-level frames[27] provided by the various controllers of the discourse.[28] As a potential solution on the complexity of issue-specific agendas, Steinberg argues that people combine media discourses, popular discourses, and personal narratives to frame political issues.

Finally, Steinberg argues that since "ideology is structured through [a] conflict-riven process of meaning, it is unlikely to be manifest in neatly structured packages or worldviews."[29] This concept provides support to the critiques of collection action framing. He also argues that in generic discourse, the power holders of the discourse attempt to define common sense understanding of complex problems. For these reasons, Steinberg suggests that instead of focusing on the ideology or belief system presented in the frame, researchers should focus on the discourse within the process. In this way, researchers can develop an understanding of the collective actors diagnosis, prognosis, and motivation.[30] This hypothesis is supported by the anecdotal description of the debate surrounding the murder of the U.S. Ambassador to Libya. Much media attention was focused on whether or not the violence in Libya was a terrorist attack or not. The Obama administration came under intense scrutiny for prudently waiting until the facts of the night became clear before they labeled it an act of terror.[31] Instead of focusing on the horrific violence, the murder of a diplomat, an attack on diplomatic property, or any of the other policy issues, the primary focus of the day seemed to center around whether a terrorist organization had masterminded the attack, as if somehow, that would explain or otherwise rationalize this seemingly senseless and random act of violence.

If collective action framing encapsulates both policy images and policy narratives for policy oriented frames, then Steinberg's critiques give light to deficiencies in research and schemata and underscore the importance of the narrative. Although his recommendations for focusing on the discourse by using social psychology analysis and a dialogic perspective may shed light on the interplay within the narrative, they do not fully answer the research questions posed earlier in the study. They do however, seem to suggest that the narrative, or to use Steinberg's term, the discourse, is required prior to mobilization for policy change at any level. They further support the theory that those in control of the narrative and in control of the images shape collective cognition of a particular policy issue.

Policy Narratives and Policy Processes

The literature previously reviewed seems to support the concept of policy images and policy narratives acting in concert to drive policy change, but do not specify a particular framework from which to move forward on understanding the relationship between a narrative and its corresponding policy. To help answer this question, Shanahan, Jones, and McBeth's article, *Policy Narratives and Policy Processes*, offer the Narrative Policy Framework (NPF) as a method for investigating the role of the narrative in the Advocacy Coalition Framework (ACF). In ACF, the narrative is one of the five foundational premises; the others being that scientific and technical information are given a central in role in the policy process, a time perspective of 10 years or more is required to understand policy change, the primary unit of analysis is the policy subsystem (policy topic, geographic scope, and influence actors), and finally, the policy subsystem actors include officials from all levels of government, consultants, scientists, and media.[32] In comparison to the ACF, these authors argue the policy narrative is more central to the policy process than scientific and technical data.[33] According to Shanahan, Jones, and McBeth, the NPF is a "holistic framework designed to accurately capture and describe policy narratives" and provides "testable hypotheses that allow for the accurate assessment of the influence of policy narratives on public opinion, policy change, and policy outcomes."[34] For the authors, policy narratives contain both narrative elements

25

and strategies to deal with policy issues. In this respect, actors, individual or collective, use words, images, and symbols to develop policy narratives which will resonate with the public, relevant stakeholders, and decision makers. The primary intent of this is to produce a "winning coalition."[35] This seems to suggest the narrative elements are likely the policy images described above and that the strategies are the mobilization affects described in both the collective action framework and the critiques offered by Steinberg.

Furthermore, the authors argue the policy environment has become incredibly "complex and cacophonous as competing policy narratives are increasing reverberating in public discourse."[36] For this argument, they suggest that policy narratives are no longer restricted to the traditional gatekeepers. New media offers fast venues and means for dissemination of policy narratives and contributes to this media din. Finally, they suggest that policy narratives are a critical source for understanding political ideologies and problem definition. As a counter to this, they recognize a competing argument that suggests narratives do little to change the course of policy making and instead are "simply fodder entertaining the masses."[37] All of this supports the claim that getting the message out is as important as crafting the message in the first place. In defining the NPF, the authors suggest that policy narratives must have a plot, with characters, and solutions, all in a generalizable context.[38] In addition to this definition, the NPF contains a handful of assumptions, such as: (1) the policy narrative is central to the policy making process, (2) these narratives operate at the individual, policy system, and institutional level, (3) a wide variety of voices contribute to the narratives, and finally, (4) policies and programs are political translations of beliefs, or policy information, organized and communicated through a narrative.[39] According to NPF, policy narratives influence policy change at three potential levels of analysis: individual (micro), group or coalition

(meso), and institutional or cultural (macro).[40] Additionally, NPF theory proposes four

categories for analysis: the specific unit of analysis, classes of variables, theoretical

causal drivers of policy change, and types of actors who motivate policy change.[41] (see

table 1).

Photo Removed Due to Copyright Restrictions

Source: Elizabeth A. Shanahan, Michael D. Jones, and Mark K. McBeth, "Policy Narratives and Policy Processes," *Policy Studies Journal* 39, no. 3 (2011): 541.

For the purposes of their study, Shanahan, Jones, and McBeth argue that the individual or micro level is still undeveloped and as such have focused their research on the group/coalition or meso level. Additionally, the authors offer a diagram to help explain how the external conditions and the various variables that influence the narrative elements affect the policy subsystem in comparison to the Advocacy Coalition Framework (see figure 2). The identification of core policy beliefs could be in essence the master frame described by the CAF theory, to which individual actors would align their policy subsystem frames or narratives. In their argument, Shanahan and her colleagues suggest that the "narrative elements of characters can reveal . . . [core] policy beliefs."[42]

In addition to these core beliefs, the authors argue that policy narratives also offer narrative strategies depending on whether the policy coalition identifies itself as winning or losing in the policy subsystem.[43] From these perspectives emerge several tactics. First, that winning coalitions seek to preserve the status quo, attempt to contain the issue by limiting the scope of conflict, and diffuse benefits and concentrate of costs. In contrast, losing coalitions seek to change the policy, expand the issue, and concentrate on benefits and diffuse the costs.[44] Additionally, the authors identify two more tactics which are likely used by a losing coalition in order to mobilize for change and widen the scope of the policy subsystem, they include policy symbols and policy surrogates. Policy symbols are emotionally charged rhetoric and policy surrogates are what seem straightforward problems aligned to more controversial problems.[45] From their research, the authors conclude that of all the components of change in either the NPF or ACF, strategy is the least studied, yet most influential component to effect policy changes.

29

Photo Removed Due to Copyright Restrictions

Figure 3.   Narrative Policy Framework Meso-Level Perspective of ACF

Source: Elizabeth A. Shanahan, Michael D. Jones, and Mark K. McBeth, "Policy Narratives and Policy Processes," *Policy Studies Journal* 39, no. 3 (2011): 543.

War Narratives and the American Will in War

The research thus far has focused on the policy narrative as it relates to policymaking, but has still not sufficiently addressed the relationship between the two. Jeff Kubiak offers in his book, *War Narratives and the American Will in War*, an excellent example of the interdependence and reciprocal nature of narratives and policymaking. While his book focuses on war narratives and war legitimation, he provides a cogent argument for a relationship structure that could be applied to the broader topic of policy narratives and policymaking.

One of the more interesting arguments proposed by Kubiak is his assertion that public support for a war policy is naturally subordinated to the policymakers. In his words, "the mass public does not make policy—the policy elites do."[46] While he concedes "public support for war must certainly contribute mightily to any understanding of stability and change in war policy," his research suggests, "foreign policy is made without much regard for public opinion."[47] This is not to say that public opinion is not important as his research further suggests that indeed it is. Here Kubiak asserts that there is a reciprocal relationship between the political elites and the public with regard to policy shifts.

He discusses two important concepts, the bottom-up and top-down model of democracy, and the ability of public opinion to keep policy initiatives near the political center of the debate. In the first concept, he asserts that policy elites take cues directly from public opinion in a bottom-up, populist model of democracy, but that elite opinion also fundamentally shapes public opinion, in a top-down model.[48] On the second concept, he asserts that public opinion "serves as a force for moderation, creating an opposing reaction to policy initiatives that stray too far from center."[49] Both of these are interesting in that they describe activity within the discourse that run counter to the belief that policy elites dominate policy narratives, but also support the concept that policy narratives can influence public opinion.

One possible hypothesis for this relationship is that policy elites, with the power to shape the policy narrative, take cues from public opinion to ensure their policy narrative is aligned with a master frame, to borrow a concept from collective action framing, and to measure the saliency of the narrative. It is also possible, as Kubiak points out, that assessing public opinion could very well be one of the first steps in policy making "wherein possible alternatives are rejected without evaluative consideration of their merits because they simply would not be able to gain or hold support from the public."[50] In this respect, Kubiak's research seems to bear out the importance of the core policy beliefs described in the NPF, and the underlying policy images described in PE Theory.

Kubiak builds on both the agenda-setting public policy analysis and PE theory of policy analysis discussed earlier to develop an understanding of the roles of the institution and the policy image. Here he asserts that for a "war policy, the policy image is communicated through a war narrative."[51] For his argument, Kubiak asserts that war narratives, narratives about the crisis, the past, the present, and expectations about the future all in context, along with its legitimating role, are central to "the sustainability of [a] war policy."[52] His contention that the role of policy legitimation is required for both the political elites and the public to ensure long-term support for a policy, sheds further light on the relationship between a policy and its supporting narrative. Regardless of the legitimation relationship, this understanding of the who, what, where, why, and how of the crisis is communicated through a narrative. In his discussion of narrative discourse, Kubiak suggests a hierarchy approach, where at the top is a master narrative, or possibly a meta-narrative, which is bounded by the society's identity, beliefs, values, and mores.[53] The next level, he continues, is the dominant narrative in the national security environment, whose primary purpose is to "define the U.S. identity relative to the rest of the world."[54] Subordinate to that of course is the war narrative, which moves the story to action. It is at this level, according to Kubiak, that the narrative's purpose is both mobilization and policy legitimation. Finally, it is important to note, that for Kubiak, the war narrative "comes analytically prior to the elites' perception of costs and benefits with regard to war policy"[55] and that it offers the perception that the problem can only "be effectively solved through the use of military force."[56] Through this specific policy subsystem, one can begin to see the relationship of policy narratives and policymaking.

Summary and Conclusions

While the authors of PE Theory offer an easy to understand framework for the complex policymaking process, their description alone is not enough to describe the relationship between narratives and policy. Like policy narratives, policy images are simplistic descriptions of one's understanding of a problem or issue. If policy images have both observable facts and a representation of what one should think of those facts, then it reasonable to suppose the policy image is communicated via a policy narrative. True, Jones, and Baumgartner, then, would seem to suggest that the policy narrative is a driver for policy change and as such, policy must be subordinated to both the underlying policy image and its corresponding narrative, or in other words, subordinated to our

33

understanding of the problem, environment, actors, and end states. The iterative and reciprocal relationship alluded to above, may be an indication of the complex relationship between policy narratives and policymaking, but PE Theory would seem to suggest that the narrative comes first. Furthermore, if PE Theory holds true, pre-existing narratives will serve only to advance the stasis or equilibrium of the policy, and only when the narrative changes, as an example during a crisis or war, will significant change in policy occur. Additionally, the converse is also likely true, that a change in policy would not generate a new meta-narrative. PE Theory would suggest that the new policy was indeed in response to a change in narrative, even if that narrative remains aligned to a meta-narrative. Finally, while narratives, and their policy images, may help to legitimize a particular policy, only those dominant and prevailing images that resonate with the policy makers and encapsulate their collective understanding and desired outcomes will support legitimacy efforts.

Unfortunately, Herrmann and his fellow scholars in their research on images and international relations did not examine the subsequent narrative following the image at play. Additionally, they were unable to determine if the images were previously conceived and matched in their experiments or if they were the result of logical conclusions about the questions used in the experiment. It does seem reasonable given the previous research that when images are developed, they are influenced from a previous understanding of the situation or similar situations. Their research does bear out that how one perceives a situation or opponent, and forms an image based on that understanding, influences the policy choices available. In this respect, their evidence supports True, Jones, and Baumgartner, who suggested that policy images come before policy decisions.

34

Unfortunately, how these images are constructed in a narrative to support, legitimate, or explain a foreign policy is still unclear.

In attempting to answer the primary and secondary research questions, collective action frame theory seems to suggest that policy narratives come before policy decisions, and that policy narratives can mobilize support and action for a particular policy. Interestingly it also describes ways in which collective action frames can legitimize action and offers an understanding where the narrative, or discourse in their terms, affects the events that, in turn, may change the underlying images.[57] Unfortunately it falls short of developing a model for examining the relationship between the narrative and the policy change.

While *Policy Narratives and Policy Processes* suggests that a policy narrative is meant to resonate with the public and produce a winning coalition, it raises two questions. First, if those with the diplomatic power to control the discourse and thus control the policy narratives, howmuch influence then, does the public have in policy decisions? And second, if the policy narrative is only intended to build this winning coalition, how does it change when the coalition falls apart without significant change to the underlying policy images or strategies as inherently described in the definition of policy narratives by the authors? Furthermore, the NPF might be enhanced with further research using more complex scenarios than two party contests. For example, many foreign policy issues are complex combinations of governments competing or working in concert to achieve a political aim. Additionally, Shanahan and her co-authors seem ready to accept the ACF argument that policy change must be examined by a period of 10 years or more. In today's new media age, it seems reasonable that one could research policy change in periods of time less than a decade long debate. Finally, while she and her co-authors recognize the important and central role of policy narratives, they conclude with the importance of strategy as the single most important component of the policy narrative. In summary, Shanahan, and her co-authors, seem to suggest that a policy narrative is required for policy change, but don't elaborate on the ability of a narrative to reinforce or legitimize that change.

If Kubiak's assertions in *War Narratives and the American Will in War* are correct, policy images, the need for legitimation, and policy narratives are collectively evaluated before policy decisions. Additionally, the policy narrative, because it was first evaluated for legitimation ability in the reciprocal relationship between the elites and the public described above, serves not only to describe the policy specific issues but also to provide long-term support for the policy. From this research, it seems as if there is a reciprocal and iterative relationship, not unlike that of the elites and the public, between the narrative and the policy.

The research here shows that there are differing opinions as to the relationship between policy narratives and policy, but in general, the narrative, based on policy images, or master frames, or core policy beliefs, comes analytically prior to policy decisions. Steven Corman, a professor in the Hugh Downs School of Human Communication at Arizona State University and an expert in strategic communications believes that in attempting to understand the relationship between a narrative and the corresponding policy, the narrative can define the problem, the desired end state, and a projected resolution, whereas the policy, on the other hand, is the mechanism to guide efforts toward that resolution.[58] His assertion that the narrative precedes the policy is supported by the research in this chapter. Additionally, this research suggests that there are many forces at work here, not just narratives and policy, by also policy images, framing, core policy beliefs, legitimation, and the relationship between policymakers and the public, to name a few. There is also likely a hierarchy of narratives from which policy makers draw on, align to, and invoke when framing the policy problem. The author then concludes the following: (1) policy narratives come analytically before policy decisions, (2) policy narratives serve as legitimation vehicles for policy before, during, and after policy decisions, and (3) policy narratives can change in response to changes in the underlying policy images or core policy beliefs. What is still unclear is the extent or manor in which pre-existing narratives drive policy change, if changes in the environment necessitate a new narrative, or if all changes in policy originate from a change in narrative? In other words, can you have a change in policy without changing the narrative? Additionally, this literature review failed to address the other secondary questions of how competing narratives might drive instability in the policy subsystem or whether or not policy, narrative, and change anlaysis can occur for periods less than ten years.

Based on the literature review above, the author also concludes that further research may help answer the remaining secondary questions. The following chapters will describe a qualitative case study methodology for answering these questions, as well as some of the concepts presented in this research above by using the recent events in Syria. This will be followed by chapters discussing the author's analysis and finally present conclusions regarding this study as a whole.

¹ Matthew C. Armstrong, e-mail to the author, October 22, 2014. Armstrong is an author, speaker, and strategist on issues related to public diplomacy, currently serving as a member of the Broadcasting Board of Governors and in 2011, he served as executive director of the U.S. advisory Commission on Public Diplomacy.

² There are many sources to indicate the number of citations a particular document has, but Google Scholar, allows one to see how many citations a particular theory has by aggregating those individual searches. In this instance, PE Theory and the documents that reference it have been cited over 3,000 times. Readers can find this information by doing a search for "Punctuated Equilibrium Theory and Policy Change" on Google Scholar: http://scholar.google.com/scholar?hl=en&q=punctuated+equilibrium+theory+policy+change.

³ James L. True, Bruan D. Jones, and Frank R. Baumgartner, "Punctuated-Equilibrium Theory," *Theories of the Policy Process*, ed. Paul A. Sabatier (Boulder, CO: Westview, 2007), 155. According to True, Jones, and Baumgartner, PE Theory "seeks to explain the simple observation that political processes are generally characterized by stability and incrementalism, but occasionally they produce large-scale departures from the past." They continue to suggest "stasis, rather than crisis, typically characterizes most policy areas, but crises do occur."

⁴ Ibid., 157.

⁵ Ibid., 159.

⁶ Ibid., 163.

⁷ Ibid., 178.

⁸ Richard K. Herrmann, James F. Voss, Tonya Y. E. Schooler, and Joseph Ciarrochi, "Images in International Relations: An Experimental Test of Cognitive Schemata," *International Studies Quarterly* 41, no. 3 (September 1997): 403-433.

⁹ Ibid., 404.

¹⁰ Ibid., 407.

¹¹ Ibid.

¹² Gideon Rose, "Neoclassical Realism and Theories of Foreign Policy," *World Politics* 51, no. 1 (October 1998): 146. "Its adherents argue that the scope and ambition of a country's foreign policy is driven first and foremost by its place in the international system and specifically by its relative material power capabilities. This is why they are realist."

¹³ Herrmann et al., "Images in International Relations," 423.

[14] Robert D. Benford and David A. Snow, "Framing Processes and Social Movements: An Overview and Assessment," *Annual Review of Sociology* 26 (2000): 614.

[15] Ibid.

[16] Ibid.

[17] Ibid.

[18] Ibid., 615.

[19] Ibid., 614.

[20] Ibid., 617.

[21] Ibid.

[22] Ibid., 622.

[23] Ibid., 628.

[24] "Bakhtin Circle," The Internet Encyclopedia of Philosophy, accessed October 27, 2014, http://www.iep.utm.edu/bakhtin/. "The [Bakhtin] circle addressed philosophically the social and cultural issues posed by the Russian Revolution and its degeneration into the Stalin dictatorship. Their work focused on the centrality of questions of significance in social life in general and artistic creation in particular, examining the way in which language registered the conflicts between social groups. The key views of the circle are that linguistic production is essentially dialogic, formed in the process of social interaction, and that this leads to the interaction of different social values being registered in terms of reaccentuation of the speech of others. While the ruling stratum tries to posit a single discourse as exemplary, the subordinate classes are inclined to subvert this monologic closure. In the sphere of literature, poetry and epics represent the centripetal forces within the cultural arena whereas the novel is the structurally elaborated expression of popular ideologiekritik, the radical criticism of society."

[25] Marc W. Steinberg, "Tilting the Frame: Considerations on Collective Action Framing from a Discursive Turn," *Theory and Society* 27, no. 6 (December 1998): 847.

[26] Ibid., 848.

[27] Levels of analysis can be generally divided along three population sizes, the micro, meso, and macro levels. Meso-level analysis falls on a population size in between micro and macro level analysis, such as a community, organization, or institution. Examples of meso-level units of analysis might include clans, tribes, communities, villages, towns, cities, organizations, diaspora, institutional subsystems, or state. Of course this list is not comprehensive.

[28] Steinberg, "Tilting the Frame," 849.

[29] Ibid., 854.

[30] Ibid., 856.

[31] CNN Wire Staff, "CNN Fact Check: A day after Libya Attack, Obama described it as 'Acts of Terror'," CNN Politics, October 17, 2012, accessed November 2, 2014, http://www.cnn.com/2012/10/17/politics/fact-check-terror/index.html.

[32] Vuechner Institute for Governance, University of Colorado at Denver, "Advocacy Coalition Framework," UC Denver Online, accessed October 14, 2014, http://www.ucdenver.edu/academics/colleges/SPA/BuechnerInstitute/Centers/WOPPR/ACF/Pages/ACFOverview.aspx.

[33] Elizabeth A. Shanahan, Michael D. Jones, and Mark K. McBeth, "Policy Narratives and Policy Processes," *Policy Studies Journal* 39, no. 3 (2011): 535.

[34] Ibid.

[35] Ibid., 536.

[36] Ibid.

[37] Ibid., 535.

[38] Ibid., 540.

[39] Ibid.

[40] Ibid.

[41] Ibid.

[42] Ibid., 544.

[43] Ibid.

[44] Ibid.

[45] Ibid.

[46] Jeffrey J. Kubiak, *War Narratives and the American National Will in War* (New York, NY: Palgrave-Macmillan, 2014), 10.

[47] Ibid., 11.

[48] Ibid.

[49] Ibid.

[50] Ibid.

[51] Ibid., 23.

[52] Ibid., 17.

[53] Ibid., 27.

[54] Ibid.

[55] Ibid., 156.

[56] Ibid., 157.

[57] Benford et al., "Framing Processes and Social Movements," 627.

[58] Steven R. Corman, e-mail to author, October 21, 2014. Corman is a professor in the Hugh Downs School of Human Communication at Arizona State University, and has served as a consultant for the Department of Defense in counter-terrorism.

CHAPTER 3

RESEARCH METHODOLOGY

Introduction

To answer the secondary questions presented in chapter two, this thesis will use a qualitative case study of the policy narratives and their construction and reconstruction over the last five years in Syria. This method of research was selected to narrow the research focus and document analysis while allowing the author to explore the complex relationship in context from a variety of data sources. Case study analysis allows the deconstruction and reconstruction of the policy narrative that would not be possible with other research methods. Finally, case study analysis is appropriate for this topic because the relationship and boundaries between narratives and policy are not clear and contextual information can help describe that relationship.

To address the questions, the author will focus on two critical points in the Syrian conflict divided into three time periods; first, the time period in the Obama administration prior to the civil unrest and ensuing violence in March of 2011; second, the time period after the March uprising and prior to the suspected use of chemical weapons in August of 2013; and finally, the narratives and policies after the August 2013 atrocities. For each time period, the researcher will attempt to define the core policy beliefs, the policy narrative elements, the policy narrative strategy, drivers of change, and finally, the types of actors motivating policy change. After this initial step, the author will then attempt to map both the meta-narrative with its core policy beliefs and the policy narrative with its policy specific beliefs for the three time periods in the Syrian conflict.

The primary research method is a documentation review of official statements made by the USG policy makers. There are several disadvantages to this inquiry. First is the requirement to explicitly clarify what information is used and searched during the discovery phase of this thesis. Second, this research reviews policy change over a relatively short period of time. Third, this research only uses data readily available in open source reporting. Despite these disadvantages, the Syrian case is uniquely interesting in that it escalated very quickly and, because of Syria's relationship with long-time adversarial governments, the policy arena is quite complex, both of which should offer some insights into the policy narrative and policy relationship.

The Narrative Exploration

Because a narrative is a fluid description of the environment, actors, and relationships, there are no sources of what a given narrative is for a given time period. Thus, the author attempts to discern the appropriate narrative from public statements and official documents for a given period. This narrative is then compared to the backdrop of events in Syria that generated the need for those statements. It has been argued that political narratives are generally bound chronologically and spatially.[1] By bounding the narrative within a chronology of events over a specific time period in Syria, the author can then build upon the literature above to develop an understanding of the policy narratives in use.

Public Opinion

While there is no simple way to measure the effectiveness or legitimation of a given narrative, the author infers the relative effectiveness based on a shift in public opinion, but realizes the research in Kubiak's book suggests the relationship between the public and policymaker is iterative and reciprocal. Admittedly, this shift could be due to a change in the situation regardless of the narrative, and while the author has no control of the questions asked these polls provide unique insight into how a narrative is received by the American people and represents the authors best assessment of the relative effectiveness of a change in narrative. The polls used in this thesis include both the Gallop and the Pew Research Center.

Sources of Information

The major sources of information include official statements made by members of the USG and senior service members, as well as official policy, doctrine, and strategy publications. Because of the rapid shift in focus in 2014 from the civil war in Syria to the terrorist threat from the Islamic State, this research and the supporting documentation will only focus on the policy narrative as it relates to the Government of Syria.

Summary

The following chapter will attempt to reconstruct the U.S. meta-narrative, foreign policy narrative, and Syrian policy narrative through an analysis of the various sources of information described above. In the final chapter, the author will draw conclusions from the analysis in chapter four and offer a summary of the research in this paper.

---

[1] U.S. Department of the Army, *The Operations Process*, 2-27.

CHAPTER 4

ANALYSIS

Even the fall of Assad will not end the conflict.[1]

— Brian Michael Jenkins

Introduction

This chapter builds on the foundational understandings of policy images, narratives, and policymaking as described earlier and examines the relationship of policy narratives and policy with respect to the Syrian Uprising in 2011 onward. Central to this research are several questions; first, to what extent do dominant pre-existing narratives influence policy decisions when the policy problem changes; second, are policy changes accompanied by a new policy narrative, aligned to a pre-existing meta-narrative, justifying or legitimizing that change; third, does policy narrative analysis benefit from reviewing policy change over a longer period than one administration; fourth, can narratives contribute to instability; and finally, can the choice of a particular narrative result in missed opportunities?

This chapter will first provide a brief background on the modern history of Syria and then begin to assess the three distinct time periods of the Syrian civil war. The first section reviews the situation update, U.S. narrative, and U.S. policy from the beginning of President Obama's administration in January 2009 through what most generally agree to be the beginning of the violent clashes between Syrian security forces and protestors in March 2011. The next section discusses the situation, narrative, and policies from March 2011 to the Syrian regime's alleged use of chemical weapons in August of 2013. The third section will review the situation update, narrative, and policies after August 2013 to October 2014. The final section will address the research questions and set the stage for the final chapter.

The Modern Syrian Story

Syria's geographic location, rich cultural history, and diverse population make it an extremely important regional power. In the immediate aftermath of World War I, France assumed control of the province of Syria through a League of Nations mandate until Syria's independence in 1946. Lacking political stability, Syria initially united with Egypt in 1958 until they too separated and the Syrian Arab Republic was formed.[2] Although periods of elected rule governed Syria in the early 1960s, by 1963 the Arab Socialist Ba'ath Party seized power and established a one-party state governed by emergency law. The power shift to military officers culminated with the rise of General Hafez al-Assad in 1970.[3] After 30 years of often-oppressive reign[4] by al-Assad and the Alawite[5] political elite, Bashar al-Assad succeeded his father as President following the elder al-Assad's death in 2000.[6] Despite initial beliefs that the younger al-Assad would introduce reform, many critics claim he has failed to deliver on his promises.[7]

January 2009 to March 2011

Arab Spring Uprisings

The phrase Arab Spring brings many connotations and evokes images of peaceful protests turning violent in far-away Muslim countries in North Africa and the Middle East. While the idea of a resurgence of ethnic and religious pride would usually be welcomed in modern states, the violent nature of these uprisings is of grave concern not

46

only for the countries attempting to maintain order, but also for their neighbors and, worse yet, may have global implications. In today's globalized world, even the smallest ripple can create a tsunami wave of strategic importance. This is the case with the embattled nation of Syria. Despite a "weak military and lackluster economy" Syria has managed to "leverage its geographic location and foreign policy" to remain relevant in regional and international politics.[8] Of particular concern for U.S. policymakers are Syria's ties with Iran, Russia, and Hezbollah.

Continued oppression in the country gave rise to sectarian protests that swept across Arab countries in what has been termed the Arab Spring.[9] These anti-government 'Arab Spring' protests came to a head in March of 2011 in the Dar'a province as protesters sought to end emergency law and corruption, and protested for freedom and democratic reform.[10] These protests started small in January, but by March had resulted in a severe response by the Assad regime as police opened fire on the protestors, ultimately leading to a brutal civil war between the Sunni-dominated rebels and the Alawite-dominated regime.[11] Amid the violent steps taken to quell a civil war, which the regime described as "foreign-backed terrorists, not domestic opposition with political aims," the regime made a symbolic concession in 2011 by "repealing the country's long-standing emergency law and revising the constitution."[12] Unfortunately, the protests and violence continued and Syria has become increasingly fractured. After three years of fighting, the State Department asserted in March 2014 that the armed-conflict between the Syrian regime and various factions fighting for reform have "taken more than 146,000 lives and displaced nearly 9 million people within the country and beyond its borders."[13]

Conflict and sectarian violence in Syria has rapidly spread across the region, which threatens regional stability, and presents U.S. policy makers with complex problems in what could be described as a chaotic environment. As mentioned earlier, policymakers use narratives to describe the environment, situation, actors, problems, and potential solutions. Ostensibly, the U.S. policy narrative on the Syrian conflict should develop a shared understanding of the historical background, current situation, and future political opportunities to shape the attitudes, and possibly behavior, of both domestic and international audiences. In essence, it should serve as a tool for policymakers to extend their influence in creating, strengthening, or preserving favorable conditions that advance United States interests, policies, and objectives and should be synchronized with all the instruments of national power.

The importance of a narrative in the Syrian conflict cannot be overstated. It exists at all levels of discourse and is evidenced by the varying literature on the subject. As an example, one piece may refer to the conflict as a revolution while another a civil war. One journal may call it an uprising while another may refer to it as the Syrian Spring. Even the image of an Arab Spring, a seasonal rebirth following a harsh winter, is slanted to one perception of the struggle for power in the Middle East and North Africa. It is the narrative over the course of the crisis that reveals U.S. policymakers understanding of this complex problem.

U.S. Narratives Prior to the 2011 Syrian Uprising

While there are many sources of policy narratives, for this research some stand out as those more representative of official U.S. policy. These include the State of the Union Address, the weekly Presidential Addresses, official statements by either the

President or on his behalf, official statements of the U.S. State Department, and various other policy and strategy documents such as the National Security Strategy. This section will evaluate these select sources of narrative from the Obama administration's first address in 2009 through those statements made until the escalation of violence in Syria in March of 2011.

The initial decade under Bashar al-Assad saw several key events. Following the September 11, 2001, terrorist attacks on the U.S. relations between the two countries appeared to be improving as the Syrian government began what could be described as cooperation with the U.S. in its War on Terror.[14] However, this relationship began to cool with Syria's opposition to the Iraq War in 2003 and U.S. claims that Syria's border was more porous than ever as a steady stream of foreign fighters flooded Iraq. This was exacerbated by Syria's interference in Lebanon and the alleged assassination of former Lebanese Prime Minister Rafik Hariri, after which the U.S. recalled its Ambassador to Syria. This period saw an increase in U.S. economic sanctions on Syria in 2004, 2005, 2006, and 2008.[15] These new sanctions began in 2004 with the issuance of Executive Order 13338 to deal with the Syrian government's policies in "supporting terrorism . . . the occupation of Lebanon, pursing weapons of mass destruction . . . and undermining U.S. and international efforts to stabilize Iraq."[16]

This untenable relationship shifted dramatically under the leadership of President Obama, who in 2010 sought to reengage with Syrian leadership. His steps included ending the U.S. travel advisory for American citizens traveling to Syria and appointing Robert Ford as the new U.S. Ambassador to Syria, the first Ambassador since the 2006 attack on the Embassy in Damascus. During this period, there were three State of the

Union Addresses (SOU); the first in 2009, the second in 2010, and finally a third in 2011, of which not a single address mentioned Syria. In fact, the problems facing the Middle East are surprisingly absent. While each of these SOUs touch on the current wars in Iraq and Afghanistan, it is only from the perspective that the U.S. policy would be to responsibly end both wars.

In Iraq specifically, the U.S. policy narrative seemed to center on returning the security responsibility of Iraq back to its people. The same is equally true of the narrative on Afghanistan. Here the President seemed committed to building an enduring relationship and security cooperation with the people of Afghanistan so that they too, may retake the security responsibility for their country. Finally, in the 2009 SOU, the President addressed the need for peace between Israel and her neighbors, and offers engagement with a Special U.S. envoy to the region as a solution. The Broader Middle East was not heavily discussed in these addresses. It appears that the majority of the policy narrative in each of these documents centers on domestic policy issues such as the economy, healthcare, medical insurance, job growth, social programs, et cetera. The foreign policy narrative focused on those countries in violation of international agreements and norms, such as North Korea's pursuit of nuclear weapons and Iran's failure to comply with its obligations, both of which warranted "tighter sanctions than ever before."[17] In all, the consistent foreign policy narratives in these documents suggested the Obama administration's desire to pursue an international solution to foreign policy problems and rely on the economic instrument of power to force compliance with international norms. The major themes in these narratives included human rights, human dignity, responsible statehood, compliance with international

50

norms, and isolation for non-compliance. It is not surprising that the President would not address a specific country in the SOU, but it is possible that the U.S. policy narrative on Syria is found in other documents.

In addition to the State of the Union, the President spoke directly to the American public in a weekly Presidential address. There were 113 weekly Presidential addresses from January 2009 until March 2011, none of which mentioned Syria, let alone their alleged sponsorship of terrorism, efforts to acquire weapons of mass destruction, their intervention in the affairs of their neighbors, mainly Lebanon, or the rising sectarian conflicts. Less than three percent of the addresses described any terrorism, protests, or violence. It is clear from this review that the focus in 2009, 2010, and the beginning of 2011 was not on Syria or Arab Spring protests. The majority of the themes and messages in these broadcasts address domestic policy issues such as the budget, economy, businesses, veterans, job growth, families, healthcare, medical insurance, et cetera. On the foreign policy front, the President's messages seemed centered on ending dependence on foreign oil and foreign influences economically. Despite being actively engaged in two war-time theaters, these weekly broadcasts address the current wars only in the context of the impact on our veterans, and America's commitment to them. However, there were two distinct themes that do stand-out in these addresses, the first is a comprehensive peace for the Middle East[18] and the second is justification of U.S. action in Libya.[19]

In September of 2009, the prospects of an Israeli-Palestinian peace appeared optimistic and the President stood resolute in his policy for engagement and dialogue with all interested parties, not just Israel and Palestine, but also their neighbors as well.

51

U.S. action in Libya, in March of 2011, prompted the March 16 Presidential address explaining and justifying U.S. the policy in Libya. In this message to the American people, the President outlined the policy as necessary to protect innocent lives from the Qaddafi regime, supporting a United Nations Security Council Resolution, and part of a broad international effort.[20]

Finally, the President evoked an emotional argument based on American values of independence and self-determination, the very values upon which this country was founded when he said,

> Every American can be proud of the lives we've saved in Libya and of the service of our men and women in uniform who once again have stood up for our interests and our ideals. And people in Libya and around the world are seeing that the United States of America stands with those who hope for a future where they can determine their own destiny.[21]

This last statement seems to indicate that as part of the U.S. policy narrative, U.S. intervention is acceptable when it defends those who seek to determine their own destiny or to save innocent lives. Rising tensions with Syria or the U.S.'s appointment of an ambassador did not make the cut for any of these addresses.

Fortunately, the SOU and the weekly addresses are not the only sources of the U.S. policy narrative. The State Department contributes heavily to the U.S. policy narrative. From this perspective, the State Department explained the President's desire for engagement with Syria as more than just talk; it is to work through the "long list of concerns with Syria"[22] while acknowledging Syria's key role in the region.[23] However, the narrative changed; when then Secretary of State Hillary Clinton condemned Syria's conviction of Syrian lawyer Haitham Maleh for exercising free speech.[24] This narrative, while different from the previous narrative, aligned with the U.S. meta-narrative on

52

supporting freedom and what Americans value as basic human rights. However, this singular instance was not enough to move the Syrian Human Rights policy issue to the high agenda. However, Secretary Clinton's remarks are consistent with the policy narratives in similar countries facing widespread protests and civil unrests. In January of 2011, Secretary Clinton addressed the event in Tunisia and asserted that those protests and demonstrations were representative of many countries in the Middle East whose people yearned "for economic opportunity, political participation, and the chance to build a better future."[25] This same narrative was echoed by the State Department regarding the protests in Algeria, Egypt, Libya, Lebanon, and Yemen.[26]

Since policy provides the end state for our strategy and policy narratives tell the story of those end states, they can also be found in the documents that guide the implementation of our strategy. There are many sources of U.S. strategy that underpin U.S. policy, however the principal document is the National Security Strategy (NSS). The NSS is a periodic document produced by the executive branch and signed by the sitting President of the United States intended to outline the major national security concerns. Despite the 1986 Goldwater-Nicholas Defense Department Reorganization Act's mandate to produce an annual report, there have been only three NSSs produced in the decade before the March 2011 uprising. The Bush administration completed one in 2004, and another in 2006, while the Obama administration completed one in 2010. For the purposes of consistency in narrative, only the 2010 NSS is reviewed in this chapter.

In this document, President Obama offered a positive view of the world in which the "circle of peaceful democracies has expanded,"[27] and one in which "the major powers are at peace."[28] However, he acknowledged the dangers of war, nuclear proliferation,

53

inequality, and economic instability.[29] The 2010 NSS identified, among other interests, the need for an "international order that promotes peace, security, and opportunity through stronger cooperation to meet global challenges."[30] However, the only mention of Syria was in reference to Arab-Israeli Peace. Here the U.S. narrative seemed centered on pursuing peace between Syria and its neighbors but does not address the Syria's oppressive regime or sponsorship of terrorism.[31] In a broader sense, the 2010 NSS described the U.S. strategy as "America's commitment to pursue our interest through an international system in which all nations have certain rights and responsibilities."[32]

With this understanding, it appears as if the narrative in play was one of open engagement to build partnerships, but not to denounce oppressive regimes. Finally, the strategy document was focused on promoting U.S. values abroad by working through international norms and not by force. If one considers Syria an adversarial government who refuses to abide by international norms, the 2010 NSS proposed greater isolation with a supporting narrative that informs the Syrian people that their international isolation is due to their government's unwillingness to reform.

However, the most intriguing part of the NSS is President Obama's discussion of Strategic Communications. Here the President stated that the U.S.,

> Must also be more effective in our deliberate communication and engagement and do a better job understanding the attitudes, opinions, grievances, and concerns of peoples—not just elites—around the world. Doing so allows us to convey credible, consistent messages and to develop effective plans, while better understanding how our actions will be perceived.[33]

This notion of understanding the environment in order to formulate policy and provide a consistent narrative was especially remarkable and insinuates that the U.S. policy narrative will be informed by the environment as the policymakers see it and help shape the environment they seek. In all, the lack of narrative on Syria within this crucial strategy document is concerning. If one were to rely solely on the 2010 NSS as a guide for dealing with democratic reform movements in Syria in 2011, then the narrative would be focused on America's commitment to recognizing the legitimacy of peaceful democratic movements, but fall short of providing support.[34]

Even as late as March of 2011, then Secretary of State Hillary Clinton believed Bashar al-Assad to be a reformer with positive intentions and distinctly different than those of Libyan dictator Muammar Qaddafi.[35] Senator John Kerry (D-Mass), then chairman of the Senate Foreign Relations Committee, insisted that the Assad regime was approachable and willing to work towards common goals with regard to peace efforts in the Middle East.[36]

In all, the U.S. meta-narrative appeared to describe the American values of: hard work and entrepreneurial spirit,[37] responsibility and accountability,[38] fairness,[39] self determination,[40] unity,[41] justice,[42] common security,[43] prosperity,[44] human dignity,[45] equality,[46] perseverance,[47] freedom,[48] resiliency,[49] and competition.[50]

Building on these, the foreign policy narrative in the Broader Middle East seemed to describe: supporting an international order, the responsible end of the wars in Iraq and Afghanistan,[51] returning governorship of Iraq and Afghanistan to their people,[52] defeating violent extremism,[53] comprehensive Israeli-Arab peace,[54] engagement,[55] support for economic opportunity,[56] political participation,[57] preventing violence,[58] and respect for the rights of all people.[59]

For Syria specifically, it appeared the narrative was that Syria is essential to U.S. support for Israeli-Arab Peace,[60] Syria plays an important role in the Middle East,[61]

America is ready to improve the U.S. Syrian relationship,[62] Assad is a reformer and his regime is approachable,[63] that the U.S. must be considerate of Iraq's neighbors,[64] but also that Syria violated international norms with regard to basic human rights.[65] This can be depicted graphically as:

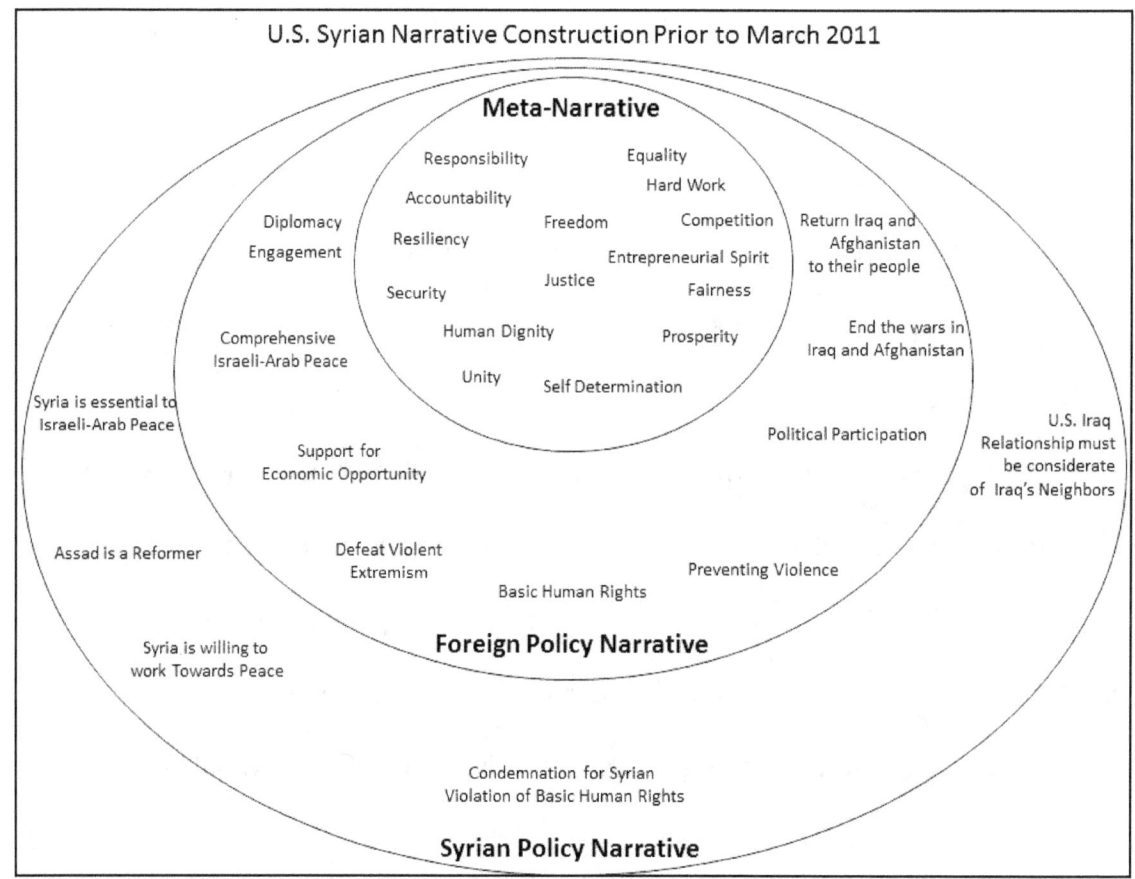

Figure 4.   Narrative Construction prior to March 2011

Source: Created by author.

U.S. Policy Prior to the 2011 Syrian Uprising

In the March 2014 Syria Fact Sheet, the State Department acknowledged that in 2009 "the U.S. began to review its Syria policy in light of changes in the country and the region, leading to an effort to engage with Syria to find areas of mutual interest, reduce regional tensions, and promote Middle East peace."[66] However, decoding that U.S. policy can be problematic. There are many sources of policy statements and policy actions available to an administration, which include official policy statements by the administration and congressional resolutions that guide the implementation of the various national instruments of power. For the purposes of this research, foreign policy documents will include executive orders, statements of policy, and congressional legislation.

While there have been a number of bills introduced in Congress, this research covered only those that became law. Admittedly legislation that was introduced but not passed by the House or Senate, or approved by the President could offer insight into the policy narrative or policy effort. However, because it was not codified as law, they may present a narrative or policy effort different than that of the administration and the collective Congress. One key area where these disparate sources of policy seem to intersect in Syria is with the economic instrument of power and the ability of the USG to sanction individuals, groups, or whole governments.

The U.S. has enforced economic sanctions on Syria under the Syria Accountability Act since 2004. Under this act, the policy of the U.S. has aimed to halt Syrian support for terrorism, end Syria's occupation of Lebanon, stop Syria's development of weapons of mass destruction, and hold Syria accountable for the "serious international security problems it has caused in the Middle East."[67] The official stated

U.S. policy in this act was that Syria should bear the responsibility for attacks committed

by terrorist groups operating out of Syria; the U.S. will work to deny Syrian ability to

acquire or develop weapons of mass destruction; Syria will continued to be listed as a

state sponsor of terrorism; Syria is interfering with Lebanese sovereignty; and finally, the

U.S. will not provide any assistance to Syria. Further, these policies would continue until

Syria ends support for terrorism, withdraws from Lebanon, and halts the development

and deployment of weapons of mass destruction.[68] Additionally, this act required an

annual presidential review.[69]

Although the Obama administration inherited this legislation from the previous

administration, this annual review enabled President Obama to support or terminate the

continuation of these sanctions. In May of 2009, President Obama reviewed this act and

found that the actions and policies of the Syrian government continued, "to pose an

unusual and extraordinary threat to the national security, foreign policy, and economy of

the United States" and elected to continue the sanctions for another year.[70] The following

year he once again continued the sanctions due to Syria's "continuing support for terrorist

organizations and pursuit of weapons of mass destruction and missile programs,"[71]

effectively extending this policy beyond the escalation of hostilities in March of 2011.

Another policy implemented prior to the Obama administration was Executive

Order 13441, issued in 2007 and pursuant to the International Emergency Economic

Powers Act. In this executive order, President Bush determined that Syrian interference

in Lebanon undermined Lebanese sovereignty and contributed to political and economic

instability.[72] This legislation blocked transactions with individuals who were determined to have taken action or posed a significant risk of taking action that would undermine Lebanese sovereignty.[73] Despite the administration's somewhat positive narrative on Syria discussed above, in July of 2009, President Obama found that "the actions of certain persons continue to contribute to political and economic instability in Lebanon" and continued the legislation for another year.[74] In July of 2010, he once again continued these sanctions for another year citing that "while there have been some recent positive developments in the Syrian-Lebanese relationship, continuing arms transfers to Hezbollah . . . serve to undermine Lebanese sovereignty . . . and continue to pose an unusual and extraordinary threat to the national security and foreign policy of the United States,"[75] once again effectively extending this policy beyond the escalation of violence that occurred in March of 2011.

Additionally, President Obama issued 39 executive orders in 2009 and 35 in 2010, but none addressed Syria. Although several bills were introduced in both the House and Senate regarding Syria, none of them became law. However, they could have represented persuasive authority, but lacked legal enforcement. As such, they were not considered statements of policy for the purposes of this research. Additionally, Syria was not addressed in any of the 47 statements of policy in 2009 or the 42 statements of policy in 2010 Overall the U.S. policies on Syria center on economic sanctions and prohibitions for Syrian citizens who were determined to have supported Syrian interference in Lebanon, Syria's sponsorship and harboring of terrorist organizations, and their pursuit of weapons of mass destruction. However, sanctions acknowledging Syria's interference in Lebanese sovereignty support for terrorism, and pursuit of weapons of mass destruction, were policy images absent from the narrative.

March 2011 to August 2013

The 2011 Syrian Uprising

In March of 2011, Syrian activists called for a day of rage inspired by other civil uprisings in Algeria, Egypt, Libya, and Tunisia.[76] This day of rage manifested in demonstrations across the country on March 18. In one of those demonstrations, in Dar'a, security forces opened fire on the demonstrators, killing five people in what has been called the first reported deadly violence in the Syrian uprising.[77] Protests and the ensuing violence continued and by April, Syrian troops were actively engaged in violently quelling anti-government protests. According to the Associated Press, thousands of soldiers opened fire on protesters in three locations killing 14 and wounding 11 more.[78] Again, in a May demonstration, Syrian troops killed another 34 people.[79] Throughout the crisis, the Assad regime used their security forces to conduct house-to-house sweeps, section off neighborhoods, and cut electricity, water, and cellphone services.[80]

By July several Syrian military officers left their posts and formed the Free Syrian Army.[81] Violence and unrest spread as hundreds were killed in the Syrian assault on the city of Hama.[82] The situation continued to deteriorate with the beating of a political cartoonist and an attack on the U.S. Embassy in Damascus by pro-regime forces in July. In September, Syrian forces killed a human rights activist in custody and other pro-regime forces again attacked Ambassador Ford's convoy. In the following February, the U.S. closed its embassy in Damascus and ordered the return of U.S. personnel. By August of 2013, it was believed that the Syrian government used chemical weapons against opposition forces. The death toll reached nearly 80,000, many of which were unarmed civilians.[83] The aggressive response by the Assad regime throughout this period

prompted a change in U.S. narratives and policy.

U.S. Narratives After the 2011 Syrian Uprising

There were two State of the Union addresses between the March 2011 uprising

and the suspected use of chemical weapons in August 2013. In the first SOU delivered in

January 2012, there were only slight changes to the meta-narrative. In this speech, the

President described additional American values of courage, selflessness, and teamwork,[84]

which was a way to further explain the previously identified policy images.

The foreign policy narrative shifted only slightly in its understanding of the

world. During this speech, the President described the U.S. as "safer and more respected

around the world,"[85] where Americans were no longer fighting in Iraq, the threat of

Osama bin Laden was no more, Al Qai'da's top lieutenants were defeated, and the

Taliban's momentum was broken.[86] He also develops a foreign policy narrative focused

on fair trade[87] that built upon the previously identified meta-narrative policy images of

fairness, accountability, and prosperity.

Additionally, the President addressed the Arab civil uprisings as "a wave of

change [that had] washed across the Middle East and North Africa."[88] In Libya, he

described American intervention as successfully removing Qaddafi.[89] In Syria, he

asserted, "that the Assad regime will soon discover that the forces of change cannot be

reversed and that human dignity cannot be denied."[90] Although he likened the Assad

regime to Qaddafi's in Libya, he stopped short of explicitly condemning the regime or

describing Assad as a dictator.[91] This narrative continued to suggest that the U.S. had "a

huge stake in the outcome" of this change, but that it was "ultimately up to the people of the region to decide their own fate."[92] He further argued that America would advocate for its values, that it would "stand against violence and intimidation," and "stand for the rights and dignity of all human beings."[93] These all build upon the previous policy images of self-determination, justice, human dignity, freedom, preventing violence, and basic human rights.

The 2013 SOU followed the same narratives as the 2012. The President's major themes in this message to the American people were that 2012 was a year of significant progress and that America was stronger.[94] He also acknowledged that there were still some challenges ahead.[95] While there are no new meta-narrative policy images, he used previously identified images throughout this address to reinforce the American narrative. On the foreign policy front, he described an Afghan led effort where American forces were returning home and the war in Afghanistan was ending, but America remained committed to "a unified and sovereign Afghanistan."[96] While he acknowledged that al Qai'da was a "shadow of its former self," he asserted that different affiliates and extremists groups had emerged and were evolving.[97] His foreign policy solutions centered on helping countries provide for their own security, but when necessary, America would continue to take direct action against those who posed "the gravest threat to Americans."[98]

With regard to Syria, President Obama asserted that America would "keep the pressure on a Syrian regime that has murdered its own people and that we will support opposition leaders who respect the rights of every Syrian."[99] From this understanding, it is easy to see how the events of 2012 have significantly changed the Syrian policy narrative. Even though this narrative changed, it remained aligned to the overarching foreign policy narratives and the meta-narrative.

Again, the President had the opportunity to address policy issues reaching the high agenda every Saturday during the President's Weekly Addresses. Between April 2011 and August 2013, President Obama gave 133 weekly addresses, none of which addressed Syria specifically. However in September of 2011, the President alluded to the civil uprising that had swept across the Arab nations. In this weekly address, the President noted, "Across the Middle East and North Africa, a new generation of citizens is showing that the future belongs to those that want to build, not destroy."[100]

While the weekly addresses did not address the growing civil war in Syria, the press releases and statements from the State Department did. During this period, the State Department played a crucial role in developing the U.S. policy narrative in Syria. Just five days after the violence in Dar'a, the State Department released a statement condemning the Syrian Government's use of violence, intimidation, and arbitrary arrests, citing that these acts hinder the ability of their people to "freely exercise their universal rights."[101] In April of 2011, the State Department called for the Syrian government to refrain from violence against and respond to the legitimate demands of their own people, while further suggesting that this was an opportunity for "meaningful political and economic reform."[102] When asked specifically if Assad had lost legitimacy in a press briefing in April, Jake Sullivan, Director of Policy Planning, declined to say as much, but instead indicated that the U.S. was strongly opposed to the course of action taken by the Syrian government and was considering tighter sanctions in an effort to force the Assad regime to end the violence and return to responsible governorship.[103]

What is unique in this narrative is the delay in describing the legitimate actions of U.S. intervention. It was only a few weeks under similar circumstance in Libya and Egypt that the U.S. intervened on behalf of the people of those two nations. A key point here is that while the circumstances were similar, the narrative was different. The argument from Sullivan was that the U.S. treats each country uniquely and that the future of Syria is up to the Syrians.[104] In this sense, the U.S. narrative seemed to imply that even after hundreds of civilians had been killed, the Assad regime could still make amends by ending the violence and opening the doors for reform.

The first evidence that the perception of Assad as a reformer had ended came in a June 2011 opinion-editorial by Secretary of State Hillary Clinton. In this piece, Clinton asserted, "Assad's violent crackdown has shattered his claims to be a reformer."[105] This narrative continued to shift throughout the year, but as early as June, President Obama said that Assad needed to lead or get out of the way.[106] By July of 2011, the narrative continued to shift away from Assad's ability to manage this crisis towards his inability to lead. In a press release, Secretary Clinton made this narrative and the underlying policy image clear when she asserted "Assad has lost his legitimacy in the eyes of his people."[107] This narrative deepened later in the month when the State Department indicated that President Assad "[was] not indispensable . . . [that] he is the cause of instability . . . and that those responsible will be held accountable for their crimes."[108] This arc continued until September of 2011, when Ghiyath Mattar, a Syrian Human Rights Activists was murdered while in Syrian Security Forces custody. Following the news of this heinous crime, the U.S. narrative included the belief that Assad must step aside.[109]

In an April 2013 briefing to the Senate Foreign Relations Committee, Acting Assistant Secretary Elizabeth Jones and U.S. Ambassador to Syria Robert Ford described the crisis as "a peaceful demand for dignity and freedom that has become one of the most devastating conflicts of the 21st century."[110] They detailed the massive human suffering of the Syrian people and the need for humanitarian assistance. Additionally, they described Assad as having lost legitimacy and as such would not play a role in a transitional government.[111] Ambassador Ford further described the Syrian regime's loss of military forces through attrition, as well as the support they received from Iran and foreign fighters. He also described the moderate opposition forces as fighting on two fronts, the regime on one side and the extremists on the other.[112]

As described above, the meta-narrative expanded slightly to include teamwork, selflessness, courage, and a stronger America. The foreign policy narrative expanded as well, to include an updated understanding of the end to the wars in Iraq and Afghanistan, the need for fair trade, the defeat of al Qai'da and the success against the Taliban, that America will take direct action when necessary, and finally, support for peaceful protestors across the Middle East and North Africa. In Syria, the narrative changed significantly. Here the U.S. narrative moved away from Assad as a reformer and toward the understanding that he had lost legitimacy and must therefor step down. Furthermore, that Assad heads a regime that murdered its own people and ignored human dignity. In response, the U.S. would stand against the violence and intimidation and support the opposition forces, but remained militarily detached, as the people of the region would decide their own fate.

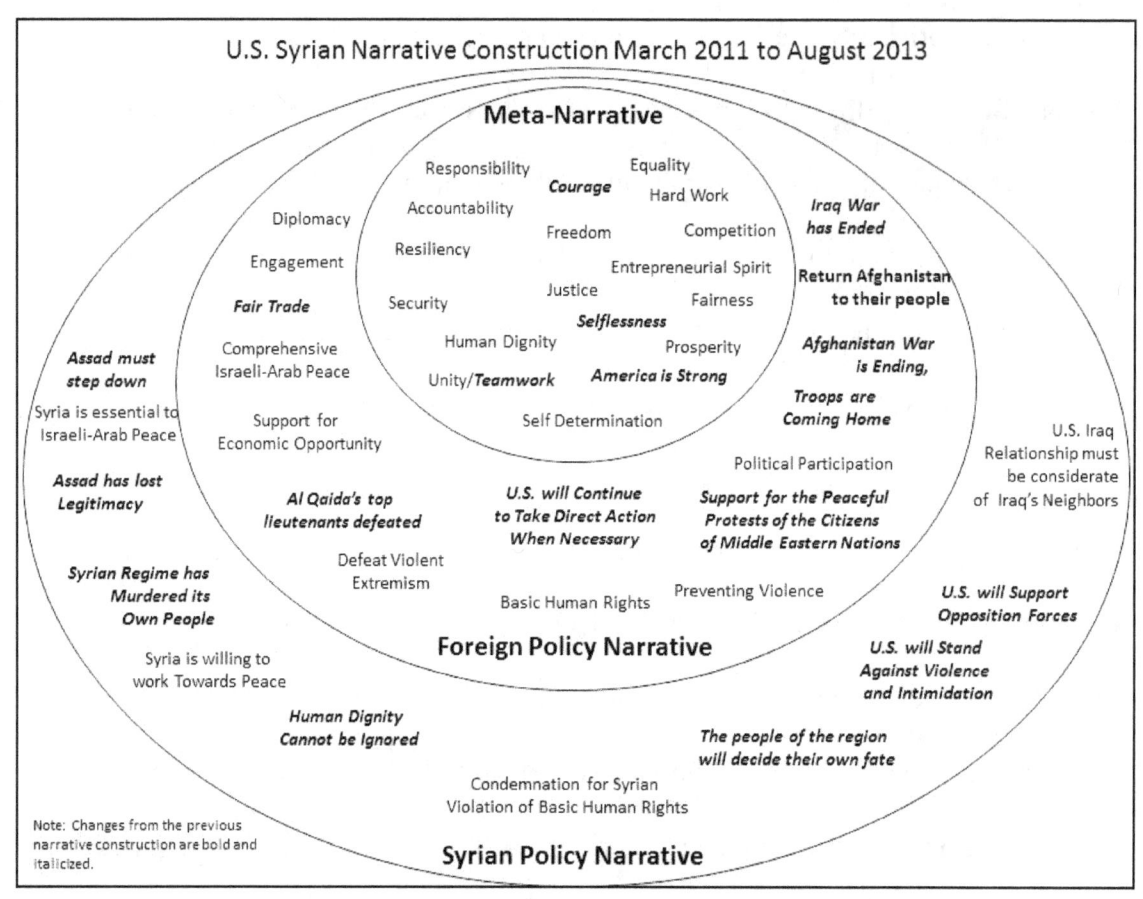

Figure 5.   Narrative Construction from March 2011 to August 2013

Source: Created by author.

U.S. Policy After the 2011 Syrian Uprising

In 2011, President Obama signed three Executive Orders addressing policy concerns with the rising crisis in Syria. The first, Executive Order 13572 "Blocking Property of Certain Persons with Respect to Human Rights Abuses in Syria," signed in April of 2011, built upon and expanded the sanctions imposed by the Bush administration. In this policy, President Obama found that the Government of Syria had committed human rights abuses, which included the repression of the Syrian people, as well as the arbitrary arrests of and the use of violence and torture against peaceful protestors.[113] This first executive order specifically identified a Brigade Commander in the Syrian Army's Fourth Armored Division, as well as the heads of two directorates and two additional entities - the Syrian General Intelligence Directorate and the Islamic Revolutionary Guard Corps, or Quds Force. The following month, the President signed Executive Order 13573 "Blocking Property of Senior Officials of the Government of Syria," which cited the Syrian Government's escalation of violence against the Syrian people, including attacks on, as well as arrests and harassment of protestors, and the repression of democratic change.[114] This sanction specifically identified President Bashar al-Assad, his Vice President, Prime Minister, as well as other senior officials. Finally, the third Executive Order, 13582 "Blocking Property of the Government of Syria and Prohibiting Certain Transactions with Respect to Syria," further expanded the sanctions to the whole Government of Syria.[115]

In 2012, the President signed three more Executive Orders regarding Syria. The first, Executive Order 13606 "Blocking the Property and Suspending Entry into the United States of Certain Persons With Respect to Grave Human Rights Abuses by the Governments of Iran and Syria via Information Technology", identified Syrian Government attempts to disrupt computers and networks, monitor and track their people electronically, and the malign use of technology.[116] This policy was designed to prevent entities from "facilitating or committing serious human rights abuses."[117] Here the named entities included communications companies Syriatel and Datak Telecom as well as the Intelligence organizations of both Syria and Iran. In the second Executive Order, 13608 "Prohibiting Certain Transactions With and Suspending Entry Into the United States of

Foreign Sanctions Evaders With Respect to Iran and Syria," President Obama found that the "efforts by foreign persons to engage in activities intended to evade U.S. economic and financial sanctions" undermine U.S. efforts to address the national emergencies declared in previous Executive Orders.[118] This broad sanction allowed the Treasury Department to identify and sanction individuals or entities seeking to subvert existing sanctions whether for their own gain or on behalf of someone else. Finally, in October of 2012, the President signed Executive Order 13628 "Authorizing the implementation of Certain Sanctions Set Forth in the Iran Threat Reduction and Syria Human Rights Act of 2012 and Additional Sanctions With Respect to Iran," further broadening the sanctions which could be applied to individuals identified by the Treasury and State Departments who failed to comply with previous sanctions.[119] Additionally, there were 15 other Executive Orders signed prior to August of 2013, but none of them addressed the Syrian crisis. The President also signed 103 statements of policy in 2011, 68 in 2012, and another 50 in 2013 prior to August. However, none of these 221 statements of policy addressed the Syrian crisis.

In April of 2013, the State Department provided an update on the U.S. policy toward Syria.[120] In this briefing to the Senate Foreign Relations Committee, Acting Assistant Secretary for the Bureau of Near Eastern Affairs Elizabeth Jones, and the U.S. Ambassador to Syria Robert Ford, outlined the current U.S. policy. According to Jones and Ford, the U.S. was pursuing three avenues of resolution. First, the U.S. had, by April of 2013, provided $385 million dollars in humanitarian relief assistance to the millions of people internally displaced.[121] This was in concert with over 40 countries that pledged a total of $1.5 billion dollars to help Syrian refugees. The second approach was partnering with the Syrian political opposition in order to facilitate a negotiated political transition.[122] Finally, the U.S. recognized that the moderate opposition was fighting two fronts, one with the Regime backed by Iranian and foreign fighters, and another against al Qai'da affiliates and other violent extremists. In response, the U.S. announced a new package of $63 million dollars in assistance for the opposition to counter the violent extremists it was fighting.[123] Towards the end of 2012, it appeared that the USG was concerned about the Syrian government's possible use of its large stockpiles of chemical weapons against opposition forces. In August of 2012, the President stated that the use of chemical weapons would be a red line for America.[124] While this initially caused controversy, White House spokesman Josh Earnest further reiterated that the use of chemical weapons would be a grave mistake and those responsible would be held accountable.[125] This de facto statement of policy was again reiterated in April 2013.[126] In this period, the narrative and the policies began to align more closely and the narrative included statements that supported the previous economic and financial policies that existed prior to the violence in 2011.

August 2013 to October 2014

Allegations of Syrian Use of Chemical Weapons

The USG alleged that on August 21, 2013 the Syrian government carried out a nerve agent chemical weapons attack in the Damascus suburb of Ghouta killing over 1,400 people including at least 426 children.[127] However, there exists the possibility that these attacks could have been carried out by some entity other than the Syrian Government. It is entirely plausible that other entities would portray or shape world events to match a policy narrative required for legitimation. As a brief example, there is credible reporting to suggest that Turkey was planning a false flag attack on Turkey or Turkish property to justify a military response from Turkey on Syria.[128] Regardless, the debate as to who actually perpetrated these heinous chemical attacks is still on going. In January of 2014, two authors, Richard Lloyd a former U. N. Weapons Inspector and Theodore Postal a professor of science at the Massachusetts Institute of Technology, produced a document that challenges the U.S. claim that these attacks were carried out by the Assad regime.[129] In this paper, LLyod and Postol's mathematical calculations suggest that given the rocket's design, trajectory, and payload, the attack could not possibly have originated from the Syrian controlled suburbs of Damascus. Here the authors propose that the administration's narrative "was not even close to reality."[130]

In response to these allegations, the United Nations Human Rights Council investigated the possible use of chemical weapons in Syria, and found that it was likely that the Syrian Government used chemical weapons in Khan Al Asal on March 19, Saraqueb on April 29, Ghouta on August 21, Jobar on August 24, and again in Ashrafiah Sahnaya on August 25.[131] They further assert that the use of chemical weapons continued well into 2014.[132] The author proposes that the United Nations Human Rights Council investigation is most likely the definitive source and accepts this version of history, but acknowledges that future investigations may prove counter arguments more likely to be true.

Throughout 2013 and 2014, the situation in Syria continued to deteriorate as violence escalated. By August of 2013, the United Nations' estimated that the death toll in Syria was in excess of 191,000 people including over 8,800 children.[133] As the security situation worsened, and with it the U.S. relationship with Syria, the U.S. ordered the closure of the Syrian Embassy in Washington in February of 2014.

U.S Narratives After the Alleged Use of Chemical Weapons

The final State of the Union address for this period was delivered on January 28, 2014. In this address President Obama reiterated the strength of America and the progress made in 2013, as well as those meta-narrative policy images that had permeated his addresses over the previous four years. However, he also added a slight change with the policy image of citizenship.[134] This recent addition builds upon the meta-narratives discussed earlier, primarily, the policy images of responsibility and accountability.

The foreign policy narrative shifted only slightly in that in this address the President asserted that in Afghanistan, "Afghan forces are now in the lead for their own security, [and] our troops have moved to a support role."[135] He also reinforced the narrative that while al Qai'da may be near defeat, the threat had evolved and al Qai'da affiliates and other violent extremist organizations had taken root in different parts of the world.[136] Additionally, he reinforced the policy that the U.S. will use force when needed, but "not send troops into harm's way unless it [was] truly necessary."[137] He also pointed to the administration's efforts to bring peace between Israel and Palestine, "to achieve dignity and an independent state for Palestinians," while reaffirming stalwart support for Israel. This slight shift in narrative builds on the U.S. meta-narratives of dignity, self-determination, but also the U.S.'s long-standing narrative of support for Israel. This new narrative was able to invoke policy images of competing agendas without painting the Palestinians as narrative villains. He also further reinforced the importance of sanctions and their coercive power in deterring Iranian efforts to seek nuclear weapons while

71

compelling them to abide by international law and norms. Surprisingly though, he threatened to veto further sanctions that might derail the U.S. Iran negotiations. This was a shift from a dominant economic instrument of power to a dominant diplomatic instrument of power.

In Syria, the President further clarified the U.S. policy supporting opposition forces. Here he asserted that the U.S. would support opposition forces that reject "the agenda of terrorist networks."[138] As a testament to the strength of American diplomacy, President Obama assured the American people that it was U.S. diplomacy, backed by the threat of force, which eliminated Syrian chemical weapons.[139] Furthermore, he asserted that the U.S. would continue to work with the international community to help bring a Syrian future that was free from dictatorship, terror, and fear. This narrative nested with both the foreign policy narrative and the meta-narrative.

Of the 80 Weekly Addresses between March of 2013 and September 2014, Syria was a topic in five. The first was in September of 2013, where the President acknowledged that earlier in August, "more than a thousand innocent people, including hundreds of children, were murdered in the worst chemical weapons attack of the 21st century."[140] He also asserted that the U.S. presented "a powerful case to the world that the Syrian Government was responsible for this horrific attack on its own people."[141] In this address, the President built on the policy images in the U.S. meta-narrative by calling it a "direct attack on human dignity" and a "serious threat to our national security."[142]

The following week, the President announced that because of the credible threat of U.S. military force, there was a possibility of a diplomatic solution and described Russia's willingness to join the international community in compelling Syria to give up their chemical weapons as a positive measure.[143] While this may seem like a shift in narrative between two distinct instruments of power, both narratives, the need for military intervention and the possibility of a diplomatic solution, were supported by existing foreign policy narratives. These narratives included the policy images that the U.S. would continue to take direct action when necessary and that international order ensuring justice for all peoples was a primary solution. The remaining weekly addresses that discussed Syria shifted from a foreign policy narrative regarding the Assad regime to a national security narrative about the threat from the violent extremist organization of the Islamic State.

Given the horrendous escalation in violence, it is expected that the U.S. narrative on Syria would have changed dramatically after the chemical attack in August 2013. In a press release, the official U.S. narrative shifted to address the use of chemical weapons in a Damascus suburb on August 21, in which 1,429 people were killed including 426 children.[144] Of particular importance in this press release was the repeated assertion that the information was credible, verified, and legitimate. One could infer that these statements were a pretext to a war narrative and used to justify U.S. or international action. This was further expanded in a September 10 press conference where the President painted a grim picture of the horrors of chemical weapons. Although unnecessarily descriptive, this demonstrates a shift in narrative, possibly away from efforts to secure a negotiated peace settlement towards a posture for military action.

> The situation profoundly changed, though, on August 21, when Assad's government gassed to death over a thousand people, including hundreds of children. The images from this massacre are sickening: Men, women, and children lying in rows, killed by poison gas. Others foaming at the mouth, gasping for breath. A father clutching his dead children, imploring them to get up and

73

walk. On that terrible night, the world saw in gruesome detail the terrible nature of chemical weapons, and why the overwhelming majority of humanity has declared them off-limits--a crime against humanity, and a violation of the laws of war.[145]

In these statements, the policy images were of an America unable and unwilling to turn a blind eye to atrocities, the need to hold those responsible accountable, and a responsibility to help secure the rights of individuals to live in peace and dignity.[146]

As an example of the narrative's importance, the subsequent debate over U.S. involvement in Syria topped the major media outlets following the attack. A Gallup poll conducted between September 5th and 8th shows that Syria emerged as one of five top concerns for the American public, increasing from zero percent before the attack to eight percent after the attack.[147] This poll was conducted just a few days before the Presidential address on September 10, 2013. A study undertaken by the Pew Research Center confirmed the impact of this shift in the U.S. policy narrative. In a December 2012 poll, only 27 percent of Americans polled believed the U.S. had an obligation to help the situation in Syria, when they added the word moral to the statement a few months later, that figure rose to 49 percent. Of note, however, was that when Pew conducted the survey again after the President's statements at the G-20 summit, but before his address on September 10, the poll showed that a majority of Americans (48 percent against to 29 percent for) did not want to see the U.S. use military strikes against Syria.[148] The following graphical depiction of the narrative policy image changes after August 2013 reinforces the argument that the narrative plays an important role in moving policy issues to the high agenda. The changes from the previous narrative reconstruction are noted in bold.

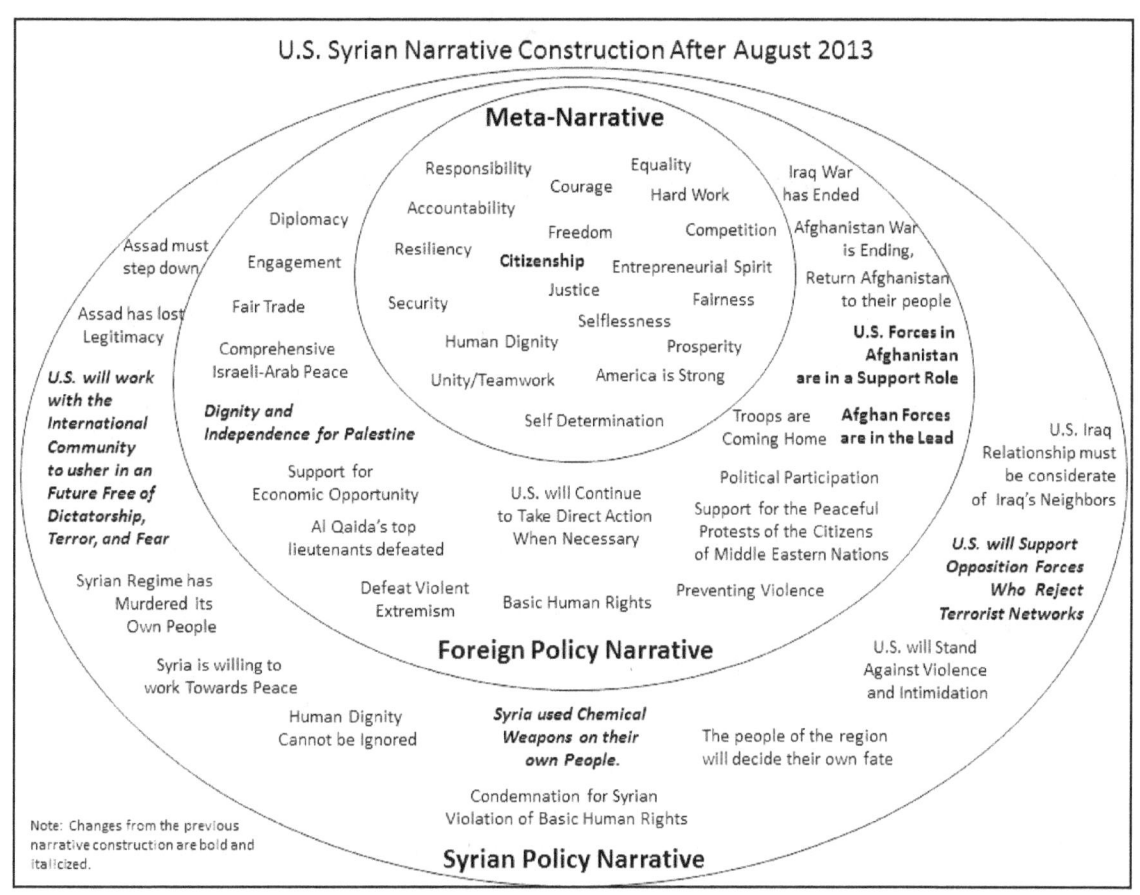

Figure 6.   Narrative Construction after August 2013

Source: Created by author.

U.S Policy after the Alleged Use of Chemical Weapons

Although not an official policy of the United States, in the initial response

following the gruesome attacks, the President stated that it was in the national security

interests of the United States to respond with a targeted military strike. It was hoped that

this strike would "deter future use of chemical weapons," "degrade the [Assad] regime's

ability to use them," and "make clear to the world that the U.S. will not tolerate their

use."[149] He also indicated that America was stronger together and as such sent the decision to Congress to debate the use of military force despite the Executive War Powers that are well within his rights as Commander in Chief. The President echoed support for military action in a weekly address when he asserted that the U.S. should take military action against the Syrian regime for their use of chemical weapons against their own people.[150] Just like his official statement, instead of invoking his War Powers authority, in this address he asked Congress to debate and vote on the authorization of military intervention.[151] By allowing Congress to debate the issue, the President appeared to be building legitimation for action through mobilization as described in the Narrative Policy Framework.

Before Congress could debate on the use of the military, Secretary Kerry was able to spur a Russian response that would lead to a diplomatic solution with the transfer and destruction of Syria's chemical weapons stockpiles. The following week, the President announced that he asked Congress to delay the vote on military intervention because of Russia's willingness to join with the international community in compelling Syrian compliance.[152]

In total, the President issued 25 Executive Orders between August 2013 and September 2014, but none of which reflected a change in the U.S. relationship with Syria or the U.S. policies towards Syria. Furthermore, between August of 2013 and October of 2014, the President issued 93 statements of policy, again none of which address the Syrian crisis.

In October of 2013, the State Department once again updated the Syrian policy and focused on two elements; supporting the opposition and seeking a political settlement.[153] According to Ambassador Ford, as of that month, the U.S. had provided over $250 million dollars in non-lethal assistance to the opposition coalition, but argued for the Syrian opposition to provide reasonable alternatives for a transition government in order to rally the Syrian people behind future Geneva peace talks.[154] On the second element, Ambassador Ford indicated that the U.S., Russia, the London 11 countries, and the United Nations all agreed that a Geneva peace conference would seek a political settlement with the creation of transition government established by mutual agreement between the opposition forces and the Syrian regime.[155] These policy efforts continued throughout the remainder of 2014.

A Longer Look at U.S. Narratives and Policy

This study attempted to narrow and focus the research by only reviewing the narratives and policies of the current administration in order to provide a single dominant policy narrative. However, if the creators of the Active Coalition Framework are correct in their assertion that one must look at policy change over a ten-year period or more, then this research would have to consider the narratives and policies of the Bush administration in the early 2000s as well. As a brief inquiry, this section will briefly evaluate the Bush administration's narrative on Syria.

Looking back on the State of the Unions from the Bush administration, it is easy to see a different dominant narrative on Syria. The first explicit reference to Syria is found in the 2005 SOU, where President Bush asserts that Syria is a sponsor of terrorism and allows extremist groups, like Hezbollah, to use parts of Syria and Syrian controlled Lebanon to disrupt the Middle East peace efforts.[156] It is in this SOU that President Bush also describes the importance of the Syrian Accountability Act discussed above.[157] In the 2006 SOU, Syria reappears as an oppressor of individual rights and freedoms and likened to North Korea and Iran.[158] Here Bush argued that America is committed to a long-term goal of ending tyranny in the world and that the "demands of justice and the peace of this world require [the Syrian citizens] freedom as well."[159] Finally, in the 2007 SOU, President Bush reaffirmed his condemnation for Syria's sponsorship of terrorism.[160] In addition to the State of the Union addresses, President Bush also offered a distinctly different narrative of Syria than President Obama's narrative in his National Security Strategies.

Although the 2002 NSS didn't mention Syria explicitly, it offers a narrative that terrorist cells have safe haven across the globe.[161] To counter this threat, Bush offered several solutions including "denying further sponsorship, support, and sanctuary to terrorist by convincing or compelling states to accept their sovereign responsibilities."[162] This narrative builds upon the U.S. meta-narrative of responsibility and accountability and would support policies, like sanctions, which sought to compel compliance. This NSS also described the U.S. efforts to "wage a war of ideas," which would delegitimize acts of terrorism, support moderate governments, and promote the free flow of information and ideas.[163] Finally, this NSS acknowledged that this would not be a quick or easy conflict, but was necessary to preserve freedom, democratic values, and the American way of life.[164] The NSS also described the U.S.'s responsibility to remain "actively engaged in critical regional disputes to avoid explosive escalation and minimize human suffering."[165] Bush continued to suggest, "When violence erupts and states falter, the United States will work with friends and partners to alleviate suffering and restore stability."[166] While this foreign policy narrative was not limited to the Middle East, Bush did elaborate on the Israeli-Arab conflict in a surprising manner. Despite the resolute support for Israel, Bush asserted, "like all other people, Palestinians deserve a government that serves their interests and listens to their voices."[167] All of this builds upon the meta-narratives of human dignity and basic human rights.

In the 2006 NSS, President Bush offered a view of the world as a nation at war. He demonstratively described Syria as a sponsor of terrorism and a tyrannical regime who combined "brutality, poverty, instability, corruption, and suffering" which threatened freedom's expansion. Furthermore, because of their sponsorship of terrorism, the Syrian regime threatened "our immediate security interests as well."[168] The strategy purposed in this document was one of ending tyranny and promoting effective democracies, but did not specifically describe those actions needed to bring Syria into international norms. This version of the NSS provided significant leeway in the policies the U.S. could pursue in Syria. Specifically, the NSS offered two broad courses of action, which included "vocal and visible steps on behalf of immediate change" and "more quiet support to lay the foundation for future reforms."[169] With regard to the Informational instrument of national power, the Bush NSS offered the following recourses: "speaking out against abuses of human rights; supporting publicly democratic reformers in repressive nations; and supporting condemnation in multilateral institutions of egregious violations of human rights and freedoms."[170] Finally, the 2006 NSS implied that it would side with reformist movements in the broader Middle East as they seek "a better life for themselves and their region."[171] In this instance, President Bush specifically stated that the U.S. would stand by the Syrian people against the "tyrannical" al-Assad regime.[172]

Narratives: Inconsistency and Instability

Covert Action and the Narrative

In attempting to answer the secondary research question of how narratives can drive instability, one should consider the USG's use of covert action. In addition to the overt policy actions available to the administration, namely the use of diplomacy and information, economic sanctions, and military intervention, covert action is another foreign policy tool available to advance national security interests. According to the National Security Act, covert action is intended "to influence political, economic, or military conditions abroad, where it is intended that the role of the United States Government will not be apparent or acknowledged publicly."[173]

One of the important considerations of covert action is that it must be sanctioned by the White House with a written finding and tempered with Congressional oversight. Once initiated, the covert action, because the activities are approved of by both the President and the Congress, becomes, in effect, policy. This type of activity could include propaganda, political action, economic action, paramilitary operations, or even lethal action. The difficulty in reconciling covert action as a foreign policy tool with the policy specific narrative is immense. Access to the findings, the congressional testimony, and the operational plans of those agencies involved in covert action are beyond the scope of this paper. However it should be noted that given the nature of covert action, there is a distinct possibility that it could be used to reinforce a narrative offered by the USG. Here some covert activities, like propaganda and political influence among others, could seek to set the conditions such that the USG desired narrative rings more true. If this is the case, it fundamentally changes the relationship between policy and narrative.

In Syria, there are a vast number of ways the President could employ covert action to help stabilize the region and coerce the Syrian regime to conform to international norms. While both administrations may have included these activities in their approach to the problem, they are likely still highly classified on ongoing. Past U.S. covert action has targeted oppressive governments with a variety of techniques and operations. Some of the more notable are the CIA's involvement in Chile 1970s,[174] the support of the anti-communist Nicaraguan Contras rebels in the 1980s,[175] efforts for regime change in Iran in the 2000s,[176] and alleged support for Laotian coup attempt in 2007.[177] Each of these would present excellent case studies as to the use of political covert action as part of a foreign policy and narrative, but also suggest that the U.S. could have employed similar techniques in Syria to help delegitimize the Syrian regime, support the moderate opposition, or otherwise influence or coerce the Syrian government to comply with international laws and norms.

However, any covert action should be weighed against the risks of escalating the violence and the threat to future human suffering. What is not clear to this author is whether the policy narrative would support these policies or if these policies would support the desired narrative. This would require further research and access to the covert action findings in order to compare them to the narrative for the given time period.

Narratives and Other Drivers of Instability

To further address the secondary question of how a narrative may drive instability, it is important to look at those potential drivers of conflict. Here again, we can use the Syrian case study to provide examples of this relationship. It may be simpler to argue that the Arab Spring uprisings were the struggle for human rights and freedoms, but there are likely other drivers for the conflict as well. Some of these drivers for instability could include drought, famine, and poverty.

Looking at the Syrian civil war, one expert suggested that Syria faced a massive, five-year drought from 2006 to 2011, where nearly 60 percent of Syria saw severe crop failures.[178] Furthermore, this drought was exacerbated by what some have described as the Assad regime's mismanagement of natural resources.[179] This level of drought led to high levels of food scarcity and even improvement in drought conditions may not have been enough to stabilize the region. Here a Humanitarian Aid foreign policy and supporting narrative may have been more effective at preventing violence in these failing and fragile states than a wait and see attitude. This would require the mobilization of wealthy international states and as such presents a good case study for the Collective Action Framework at the macro level. As the drought and famine worsened in Syria, millions migrated to urban areas and added to the economic instability across the country.[180] Finally, poverty was also a likely driver of the Syrian conflict. One expert believes that prior to the civil war, there was a population/resource ratio out of balance.[181] It is likely that Syria's dust bowl experience removed the topsoil and contributed to the worsening economic conditions. These natural conditions combined with their poor oil quality, expensive refining processes, and a falling gross domestic product, to produce a highly fragile state leading to instability.[182]

These failing and fragile states present transnational security problems and when coupled with non-state actors, like violent extremists organizations, these areas become rich sources of conflict. This was certainly true in Syria. Recognizing the dangers of drought, famine, and poverty, are just the first step in preparing the policy narrative and policy. However, both the American meta-narrative and foreign policy narratives would support policy narratives seeking to combat these other drivers of instability. A policy of humanitarian aid, or other support as required to end human suffering, support for human dignity, and provisions for the basic rights of individuals regardless of their citizenship would have nested with the U.S. meta and foreign policy narratives as well. The resulting question then becomes how does a foreign narrative of drought, famine, and poverty elevate those concerns in the U.S. to the high agenda such that U.S. policymaker's now take on those narratives as drivers for policy change? In essence, when does a narrative become the tool for action? Unfortunately further research to discover this understanding is required.

Inconsistent Narratives and Missed Opportunities

Finally, in order to answer the secondary research question of how inconsistent narratives lead to missed opportunities and to develop lessons learned for future narrative construction and policymaking, one must consider any missed opportunities in this case study. It is easy to offer critique in hindsight, but by looking at the Syrian case study, one can develop an understanding of how these missed opportunities could arise in a more general sense.

The research in this paper suggests that the administration missed several key opportunities to address both the wide spread Arab uprisings as well as the escalating tensions and ensuing violence in Syria. The absence of a Syrian policy narrative prior to the March 2011 uprising indicates that while Syria might have be considered essential to a Broader Middle East peace, it did not warrant inclusion into the high agenda. The deteriorating economic and security situation in Syria should have placed it on the table

83

for discussion with both the political elite and the public masses. The administration and the State Department had ample opportunities to bring these policy challenges to elite discourse but, unfortunately, other policy issues took precedence. A policy narrative that focused on human suffering, human dignity, freedoms, and basic human rights would have been successfully aligned with the policy images in the American meta-narrative and over arching foreign policy narratives. These narratives could have been used to generate and mobilize international support to meet the challenges in a pre-civil war Syria. Therefor, future policymakers should consider addressing failing and fragile states who have the potential to develop these drivers of instability. Advocates for policies supporting these states could make a successful argument nested not only in the U.S. narratives but also in the narratives of these key foreign audiences.

Another missed opportunity came at the outset of the 2011 violence. While the policymakers may have initially indicated that the Syrian regime was different from the Qaddafi regime, history shows that the two were more similar than different. Both regimes sponsored terrorism, attempted to intervene in the sovereignty of their neighbors, and pursued weapons of mass destruction. Both led oppressive security operations that infringed upon the freedoms and basic human rights of their citizens. As such, a Syrian policy narrative more similar to that of Libya, may have reinforced credibility and trust in U.S. policymakers. A narrative, similar to that of Libya, may also have driven more effective policies for quelling the violence, ending human suffering, and opening the doors for political reform. The lesson for future policymakers here is one of consistency. It may be easier to suggest that each country, each non-state actor, each individual is different and thus requires a different approach, but the inconsistency in narrative

84

generates a collective cognitive dissonance for the various audiences. As such, future policymakers should consider how these potentially similar circumstances are different and take the time necessary to fully develop a narrative that is either consistent with past actions or allays the concerns of those who argue the similar circumstances warrant similar policies.

Finally, after the use of chemical weapons, it was clear that the Assad regime did not respect international values and laws. This was a significant opportunity for the U.S., where the U.S. could have taken the lead in the battle of narratives, but instead yielded to Russia's influence. Certainly at the time, this appeared as the solution with the highest probability of success, but the continued use of chemical weapons through 2014 suggests that stronger condemnation and further USG policy was needed. Again, the lesson here is one of consistency. It is hard to argue against intervention in Syria where the USG alleged the regime used chemical weapons, when supposedly just a decade earlier, the U.S. invaded Iraq for potential use of chemical weapons. Just as described above, future policymakers should consider the past actions in similar circumstances and either address them sufficiently or consider similar policy narratives and actions.

Answering the Question

Despite the tumultuous turn of events and the subsequent shifts in narrative and policy, it is still not clear from this case study if pre-existing meta-narratives and higher echelon narratives influence policy decisions when the policy problem changes. What seems clear to this author is that regardless of the new subordinate narrative, in this case the Syrian narrative, it will likely be built upon those meta-narrative and higher echelon narrative policy images.

This research also suggests three additional observations. First, that the Syrian narrative prior to 2011 suggests that the U.S. Syria relationship did not warrant movement to the high agenda. Second, that a policy not supported by a corresponding narrative, for example the policy of sanctions for state sponsored terrorism without a corresponding condemnation narrative, creates uncertainty, and erodes trust in the policymakers. Finally, the arc in the narrative suggests that our perception of the world is potentially influenced by the world we seek. In a way this could be a collective cognitive bias similar to confirmation bias or optimism bias, which are experienced at the individual level. Throughout this time period, the U.S. Syrian narrative experienced a dramatic change. This arc can be represented by the simple graphic below.

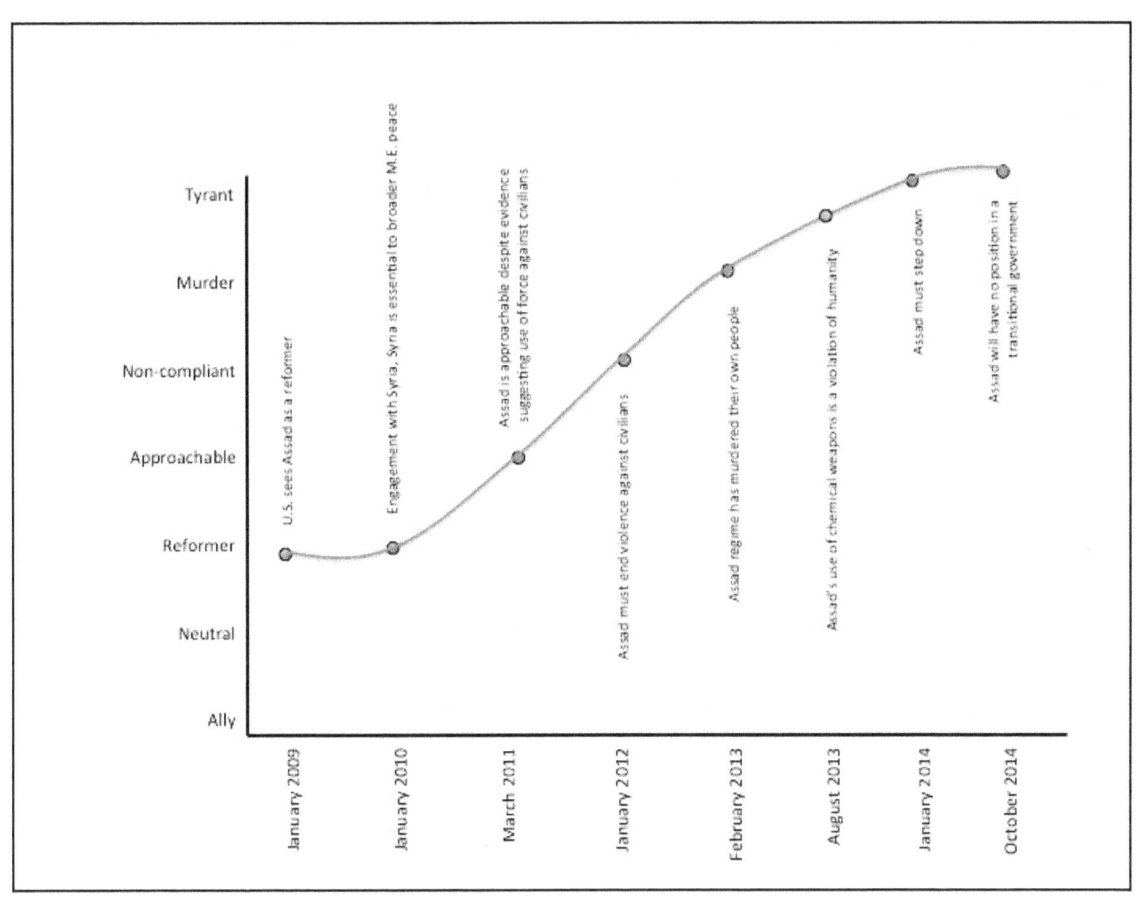

Figure 7.   Narrative Arc January 2009 to October 2014

Source: Created by author.

Looking back on the literature reviewed, it appears that Waller was correct in his

assertion that the U.S. narrative should offer a positive vision of hope and opportunity

while isolating and marginalizing violent extremists and fostering a sense of common

interests and common values. This case study also supported the PE Theory assertion that

significant change in narrative will occur from crisis. This is evidenced in that the

narrative prior to 2011 supported the stasis of the policy of the USG's Syrian policy.

Furthermore, it supported PE Theory's assertion that institutions, or venues in their terms, can block policy change, as was the case with Congress and the continuing policy of economic sanctions.

Additionally, the authors of *Images in International Relations* are also likely correct in that a policymaker's construction of reality is the foundation for policy decisions. Here perceived opportunity for public support and general war weariness outweighed the perceived threat and may have delayed U.S. policy changes that would have been more successful in quelling the violence. It was not the author's intent to critique the policy or strategy employed, but merely to understand the impediments to policy decision. As for Steinberg's critique of collective action framing, this case study makes an argument that the various ideologies are pre-existing, while the dominant ideology emerges in response to a crisis.

This case study is difficult to apply to the NPF as it only addresses the U.S. policy narratives and core policy beliefs. In order to adequately address the narrative strategies and tactics discussed in NPF theory, one would need to look at both the existing and proposed U.S. narratives. This would require reviewing testimony and introduced legislation that did not get approved by the House or Senate. Unfortunately, this is beyond the scope of the paper, but the NPF does provide some insight into the change in the official U.S. narrative. Here, one can see the elements of the policy narrative quite clearly. The characters are Assad and his regime, the peaceful protestors, the opposition forces, and the innocents who have lost their lives in this brutal civil war.

The plot becomes clearer, too, as the narrative moves into the high agenda. Here one can see the need first for reform, then regime change. One can also see the role of the international community and some of its independent plots; Russia's help to rid Syria of chemical weapons, as well as Turkey and Jordan's effort to relieve the human suffering of refugees. Finally, President Obama described the Assad regime as the causal mechanism for the violence. The policy narrative strategy becomes a bit more complicated in that if the administration is seeking policy change, then NPF would describe the administration as losing coalition where the they seek to expand the issue and concentrate on the benefits while diffusing the costs. Unfortunately the author believes the terms winning and losing might be a misnomer in that winning coalitions can certainly lose to policy change.

What is more likely is Kubiak's proposal that policies are first evaluated for legitimation prior to implementation. Here one can see the President announce to the public that he knows America is war weary and not willing to get in the middle of someone else's war, but proposes military action as necessary. Finally, this case study also supports both Kubiak's assertion that public opinion can serve as a force of moderation for policies and his theories on the reciprocal nature of the relationship between the political elite and the public.

With regard to the remaining secondary questions, this research suggests that there are other policy tools available that may or may not be supported by the overt policy narrative. Regardless, the research suggests that the narrative in play must be emotionally resonant with the target audience, true, and logical. Additionally, there are other drivers of instability that the U.S. narrative addresses. How these core grievances get elevated to the high agenda is still unclear from this research. What is clear, however, is that there are opportunities to address these drivers of instability with narrative that builds upon the policy images in the U.S. meta-narrative and foreign policy narrative.

Finally, as in any discipline, learning from the lessons of history can provide valuable insight into narrative analysis. By reviewing several key missed opportunities, future narrative construction and policymaking can learn from these missed opportunities in a way to inform future decisions.

Summary and Conclusions

In attempting to answer the remaining research questions, the author deconstructed and reconstructed the U.S. narrative with regard to the Syrian civil war. In the simplest terms a narrative is a story that describes the environment, the situation, the actors, and the preferred outcome all of which is designed to give meaning to the targeted audience and explain why the narrative is important to the policy. In this case study, it is possible to see how the narrative shifted to describe the chaotic environment, the actors both good and bad, and preferred outcomes. Furthermore, when narratives and their associated end-states are disparate, it presents further complications for policymakers in an already challenging environment.

A consistent narrative is required for the United States to help bring stability to the Levant and surrounding region and to deescalate the violence both in Syria and that which is spilling out. Because the policy narrative is tied to policy, and in this case the U.S. foreign policy in Syria, one may be tempted to assert that our narrative is inconsistent because our policy is inconsistent. However, it is possible, that U.S. strategy for pursuing an international order to promote peace remains, but the U.S. narrative fluctuates wildly with any number of influences such as public opinion, policymaker willingness for involvement, international support, etc. When the U.S. narrative in Syria was inconsistent, these inconsistencies could have hindered U.S. actions ultimately leading to the growth of violent extremist organizations that stand poised to rapidly

disrupt regional security efforts.

The next and final chapter will offer conclusions based on the research conducted

and provide a summary of the paper in its entirety.

---

[1] Brian Michael Jenkins, "The Dynamics of Syria's Civil War" (Santa Monica, CA: RAND Corporation, 2014), accessed August 13, 2014, http://www.rand.org/pubs/ perspectives/ PE115.html. In his research article for the RAND Corporation, Jenkins' asserts that the inability to win decisively in this asymmetric war will continue the political stalemate. He further suggests that even the fall of Assad and his Ba'ath Party government would not end this conflict.

[2] Central Intelligence Agency, "Syria," The World Factbook, accessed August 13, 2014, https://www.cia.gov/library/publications/the-world-factbook/geos/sy.html.

[3] Freedom House, "Syria," *Freedom in the World*, 2013, accessed August 13, 2014, http://www.freedomhouse.org/report/freedom-world/2014/syria-0#.U_agp0uQYYU.

[4] Freedom House, *Freedom in the World*, 2014, accessed October 7, 2014, www.freedomhouse.org. Starting in 1999, Freedom House has continually asserted that Syria's ruling party has used its power to oppress the Syrian populace and it has continually scored the worst ratings given by the organization.

[5] Alawite is a Shia sect of Islam, but is a minority religious group in Syria. This sect serves as the power base for the Ba'ath party that rules the country.

[6] Central Intelligence Agency, "Syria."

[7] Human Rights Watch, "Syria: President Assad Fails to Deliver Reform," March 30, 2011, accessed October 7, 2014, http://www.hrw.org/news/2011/03/30/syria-president-asad-fails-deliver-reform.

[8] Jeremy M. Sharp, *Syria: Issues for the 112th Congress and Background on U.S. Sanctions* (Washington, DC: Congressional Research Service, 2011). This research paper is prepared for members and committees of Congress and was produced within a month of the devastating class of Syrian government forces and anti-government rebels.

[9] Marc Lynch, "Obama's Arab Spring?" *Foreign Policy*, January 6, 2011, accessed August 13, 2014, http://mideastafrica.foreignpolicy.com/posts/2011/01/06/ obamas_arab_spring.

[10] Central Intelligence Agency, "Syria."

[11] The Heritage Foundation, "Syria," *The 2014 Index of Economic Freedom*, accessed August 28, 2014, http://www.heritage.org/index/country/syria. The Heritage Foundation's 2014 index looks at Syria's economy (population, GDP, inflation, business, trade, FDI, and corruption). While the numerical grading of Syria's economy remains suspended due to the on-going conflict, the Heritage Foundation still reports key facts regarding multiple facets of Syria's economy.

[12] Freedom House, "Syria."

[13] U.S. Department of State, "U.S. Relations with Syria," March 20, 2014, accessed October 14, 2014, http://www.state.gov/r/pa/ei/bgn/3580.htm.

[14] Reese W. Erlich, *Conversations with Terrorists: Middle East Leaders on Politics, Violence, and Empire* (San Francisco: PoliPointPress, 2010).

[15] Department of the Treasury, *Syria Sanctions Program*, August 2, 2013, 3, accessed October 7, 2014, http://www.treasury.gov/resource-center/sanctions/ Programs/Documents/syria.pdf.

[16] Ibid.

[17] Barrack Obama, *Address Before a Joint Session of the Congress on the State of the Union*, The American Presidency Project, February 24, 2009, accessed October 17, 2014, http://www.presidency.ucsb. edu/ws/index.php?pid=85753.

[18] Barack Obama, *The President's Weekly Address*, The American Presidency Project, September 26, 2009, accessed October 17, 2014, http://www.presidency.ucsb. edu/satradio.php.

[19] Barack Obama, *The President's Weekly Address*, The American Presidency Project, March 16, 2011, accessed October 17, 2014, http://www.presidency.ucsb.edu/ satradio.php.

[20] Ibid.

[21] Ibid.

[22] Jeffrey D. Feltman, "U.S.-Syria Relations Press Conference," U.S. Department of State, March 6, 2009, accessed November 2, 2014, http://www.state.gov/p/nea/rls/rm/ 2009/120084.htm.

[23] Ibid.

[24] Hillary R. Clinton, "Syrian Convictions of Human Rights Activists Press Conference," U.S. Department of State, July 5, 2010, accessed November 2, 2014, http://www.state.gov/secretary/20092013clinton/rm/2010/07/143966.htm.

[25] Hillary R. Clinton, "Recent Events in Tunisia in a Press Statement," U.S. Department of State, January 14, 2011, accessed November 2, 2014, http://www.state.gov/secretary/20092013clinton/rm/2011/01/154684.htm.

[26] Philip J. Crowley, "Protests in Algeria in a Press Statement," U.S. Department of State, February 13, 2011, accessed November 2, 2014, http://www.state.gov/r/pa/prs/ps/2011/02/156515.htm; Philip J. Crowley, "Situation in Egypt in a Press Statement," U.S. Department of State, January 25, 2011, accessed November 2, 2014, http://www.state.gov/r/pa/prs/ps/2011/01/155307.htm; Philip J. Crowley, "Situation in Algeria in a Press Statement," U.S. Department of State, February 20, 2011, accessed November 2, 2014, http://www.state.gov/r/pa/prs/ps/2011/02/156829.htm; Philip J. Crowley, "Situation in Lebanon in a Press Statement," U.S. Department of State, January 25, 2011, accessed November 2, 2014, http://www.state.gov/r/pa/prs/ps/2011/01/155303.htm; Hillary R. Clinton, "Violence in Yemen in a Press Statement," U.S. State Department, March 18, 2011, accessed November 2, 2014, http://www.state.gov/secretary/20092013clinton/rm/2011/03/158597.htm.

[27] Barack Obama, *National Security Strategy* (Washington, DC: The White House, 2010), 1.

[28] Ibid.

[29] Ibid.

[30] Ibid., 7.

[31] Ibid., 26.

[32] Ibid.

[33] Ibid.

[34] Ibid.

[35] Patrick Goodennough, "Syrian President Assad Regarded as a 'Reformer,' Clinton Says." *CBS News*, March 28, 2011, accessed October 7, 2014, http://cnsnews.com/news/article/syrian-president-assad-regarded-reformer-clinton-says.

[36] Ibid.

[37] Obama, *State of the Union*, February 24, 2009.

[38] Ibid.

[39] Ibid.

[40] Barack Obama, *Address Before a Joint Session of the Congress on the State of the Union*, The American Presidency Project, January 25, 2011, accessed October 30, 2014, http://www.presidency.ucsb.edu/ws/?pid=88928.

[41] Obama, *State of the Union*, February 24, 2009; Barack Obama, "Address Before a Joint Session of the Congress on the State of the Union," January 27, 2010, The American Presidency Project, accessed October 30, 2014, http://www.presidency.ucsb.edu/ws/?pid=87433. Obama, *State of the Union*, January 25, 2011.

[42] Obama. *State of the Union,* February 24, 2009.

[43] Obama, *State of the Union*, January 27, 2010.

[44] Ibid.

[45] Obama. *State of the Union*, February 24, 2009.

[46] Obama: *State of the Union*, January 27, 2010.

[47] Obama. *State of the Union*, February 24, 2009; Obama, *State of the Union*, January 27, 2010; Obama, *State of the Union*, January 25, 2011.

[48] Obama: *State of the Union*, January 25, 2011.

[49] Obama, *State of the Union*, January 27, 2010.

[50] Ibid.

[51] Obama. *State of the Union*, February 24, 2009.

[52] Obama, *State of the Union*, January 27, 2010; Obama, *State of the Union*, January 25, 2011.

[53] Obama, *State of the Union*, February 24, 2009; Obama, *State of the Union*, January 25, 2011.

[54] Obama, *State of the Union*, February 24, 2009.

[55] Obama, *State of the Union*, January 27, 2010; Obama, *State of the Union*, January 25, 2011.

[56] Clinton, "Recent Events in Tunisia," January 14, 2011.

[57] Clinton, "Recent Events in Tunisia," January 14, 2011; Crowley, "Situation in Egypt," January 25, 2011.

[58] Clinton, "Recent Events in Tunisia," January 14, 2011; Crowley, "Situation in Lebanon in a Press Statement," January 25, 2011; Crowley, "Situation in Egypt," January 25, 2011.

[59] Clinton, "Recent Events in Tunisia," January 14, 2011; Crowley, "Situation in Egypt," January 25, 2011.

[60] Obama, *National Security Strategy.* 2010; Jeffrey D. Feltman, "Acting Assistant Secretary Feltman Briefs on Meetings with Syrian Officials," U.S. Department of State, March 7, 2009, accessed November 2, 2014, http://www.state.gov/r/pa/prs/ps/2009/03/120122.htm.

[61] William J. Burns, "Remarks on middle East Peace Following Meeting with Syrian President Bashar al-Assad," U.S. Department of State, February 17, 2010, accessed November 2, 2014, http://www.state.gov/p/us/rm/2010/136717.htm.

[62] Ibid.

[63] Goodennough. "Syrian President Assad Regarded as a Reformer," March 28, 2011.

[64] Chairman, Joint Chiefs of Staff, *National Military Strategy* (Washington, DC 2010), 11-12.

[65] Clinton, "Syrian Convictions of Human Rights Activists," July 5, 2010.

[66] Bureau of Near Eastern Affairs, "U.S. Relations With Syria Fact Sheet," U.S. Department of State, March 20, 2014, accessed November 2, 2014, http://www.state.gov/r/pa/ei/bgn/3580.htm.

[67] U.S. Congress, *Syria Accountability and Lebanese Sovereignty Act of 2003,* H. Res. 1828, 108th Cong., December 12, 2003, accessed October 14, 2014, https://www.govtrack.us/congress/ bills/108/hr1828/text.

[68] Ibid.

[69] Ibid.

[70] Barack Obama, *Notice on Continuation of the National Emergency With Respect to the Actions of the Government of Syria*, The American Presidency Project, May 7, 2009, accessed November 2, 2014, http://www.presidency.ucsb.edu/ws/?pid=86115.

[71] Barack Obama, *Message to the Congress on Continuation of the National Emergency With Respect to the Actions of the Government of Syria*, The American Presidency Project, May 3, 2010, accessed November 2, 2014, http://www.presidency.ucsb.edu/ws/?pid=87896.

[72] George W. Bush, Executive Order 13441, *Blocking Property of Persons Undermining the Sovereignty of Lebanon or Its Democratic Processes and Institutions*, The American Presidency Project, August 1, 2007, accessed November 2, 2014, http://www.presidency.ucsb.edu/ws/?pid=75641.

[73] Ibid.

[74] Barack Obama, *Notice on Continuation of the National Emergency With Respect to the Actions of Certain Persons To Undermine the Sovereignty of Lebanon or Its Democratic Processes and Institutions*, The American Presidency Project, accessed November 2, 2014, July 30, 2009, http://www.presidency.ucsb.edu/ws/?pid=86480.

[75] Barack Obama, *Notice: Continuation of the National Emergency With Respect to the Actions of Certain Persons To Undermine the Sovereignty of Lebanon or Its Democratic Processes and Institutions*, The American Presidency Project, July 29, 2010, accessed November 2, 2014, http://www.presidency.ucsb.edu/ws/?pid=88257.

[76] Associated Press, "Syrian Uprising Timeline of Key Events," September 4, 2013, accessed November 2, 2014, http://www.politico.com/story/2013/09/syria-timeline-96270.html.

[77] Ibid.

[78] Ibid.

[79] Borzou Daragahi and Alexandra Sandels, "Syrian Troops Fire on Protesters, 34 Killed," *Los Angeles Times*, May 20, 2011, accessed November 2, 2014, http://articles.latimes.com/2011/may/20/world/la-fg-syria-protests-kurds-20110521.

[80] Associated Press, "Timeline of Key Events," September 4, 2013.

[81] World Tribune, "Defecting troops from 'Free Syrian Army', target Assad Security Forces," August 3, 2011, accessed November 2, 2014, http://www.worldtribune.com/worldtribune/WTARC/2011/me_syria0973_08_03.asp.

[82] Associated Press, "Timeline of Key Events," September 4, 2013.

[83] Syrian Martyrs, "Martyr Counts by Month," accessed November 2, 2014, http://syrianshuhada.com/default.asp?lang=en&a=st&st=8. The total number of deaths reported from March of 2011 through August of 2013 by *Syrian Martyrs* is 79,790.

[84] Barack Obama, *Address Before a Joint Session of Congress on the State of the Union*, The American Presidency Project, January 24, 2012, accessed November 2, 2014, http://www.presidency.ucsb.edu/ws/?pid=99000.

[85] Ibid.

[86] Ibid.

[87] Ibid.

[88] Ibid.

[89] Ibid.

[90] Ibid.

[91] Ibid. President Obama draws an connection between Qaddafi and Assad as dictators but stops short of referring to the Assad regime as a dictator. Nor does he propose a solution to the problem.

[92] Ibid.

[93] Ibid.

[94] Barack Obama, *Address Before a Joint Session of Congress on the State of the Union*, The American Presidency Project, February 12, 2013, accessed November 2, 2014, http://www.presidency.ucsb.edu/ws/index.php?pid=102826.

[95] Ibid.

[96] Ibid.

[97] Ibid.

[98] Ibid.

[99] Ibid.

[100] Barack Obama, *The President's Weekly Address,* The American Presidency Project, September 10, 2011, accessed November 2, 2014, http://www.presidency.ucsb.edu/ws/?pid=96668.

[101] Mark C. Toner, "Violence in Syria," U.S. Department of State, March 23, 2011, accessed November 2, 2014, http://www.state.gov/r/pa/prs/ps/2011/03/158894.htm.

[102] Hillary R. Clinton, "Remarks at Press Availability," U.S. Department of State, April 15, 2011, accessed November 2, 2014, http://www.state.gov/secretary/20092013 clinton/rm/2011/04/160998.htm.

[103] Jake Sullivan, "Briefing on Recent Developments in the Middle East and Other Issues," U.S. Department of State, April 26, 2011, accessed November 2, 2014, http://www.state.gov/p/nea/rls/rm/161818.htm.

[104] Ibid.

[105] Hillary R. Clinton, "Secretary Clinton Supports Syrian People in Op-Ed," U.S. Department of State, June 17, 2011, accessed November 4, 2014, http://www.state.gov/r/pa/prs/ps/2011/06/166488.htm.

[106] U.S. State Department, "Background Briefing by Senior Administration Officials on Syria," accessed November 4, 2014, June 17, 2011, http://www.state.gov/p/nea/rls/rm/166484.htm.

[107] Hillary R. Clinton, "Remarks on Libya and Syria," U.S. Department of State, July 15, 2011, accessed November 6, 2014, http://www.state.gov/secretary/20092013clinton/rm/2011/07/168656.htm.

[108] Victoria Nuland, "U.S. Condemns Ongoing Violence in Syria," U.S. Department of State, July 25, 2011, accessed November 6, 2014, http://www.state.gov/r/pa/prs/ps/2011/07/169069.htm.

[109] Victoria Nuland, "Killing of Syrian Human Rights Activist Ghiyath Matter," U.S. Department of State, September 11, 2011, accessed November 6, 2014, http://www.state.gov/r/pa/prs/ps/2011/09/172085.htm.

[110] Elizabeth Jones and Robert S. Ford, "U.S. Policy Toward Syria, Senate Foreign Relations Committee," U.S. Department of State, April 11, 2013, accessed November 2, 2014, http://www.state.gov/p/nea/rls/rm/2013/207416.htm.

[111] Obama, *Weekly Address*, September 10, 2011.

[112] Ibid.

[113] Barack Obama, Executive Order 13572, *Blocking Property of Certain Persons With Respect to Human Rights Abuses in Syria* (Washington, DC: The White House, April 2011), accessed November 2, 2014, http://www.gpo.gov/fdsys/pkg/FR-2011-05-03/pdf/2011-10910.pdf.

[114] Barack Obama, Executive Order 13573, *Blocking Property of Senior Officials of the Government of Syria* (Washington, DC: The White House, May 2011), accessed November 2, 2014, http://www.gpo.gov/fdsys/pkg/FR-2011-05-20/pdf/2011-12645.pdf.

[115] Barack Obama, Executive Order 13582, *Blocking Property of the Government of Syria and Prohibiting Certain Transactions With Respect to Syria* (Washington, DC: The White House, August 2011), accessed November 2, 2014, http://www.gpo.gov/fdsys/pkg/FR-2011-08-22/pdf/2011-21505.pdf.

[116] Barack Obama, Executive Order 13606, *Blocking Property and Suspending Entry Into the United States of Certain Persons With Respect to Grave Human Rights abuses by the Governments of Iran and Syria via Information Technology* (Washington, DC: The White House, April 2012), accessed November 2, 2014, http://www.gpo.gov/fdsys/pkg/FR-2012-04-24/pdf/2012-10034.pdf.

[117] Ibid.

[118] Barack Obama, Executive Order 13608, *Prohibiting Certain Transactions With and Suspending Entry Into the United States of Foreign Sanctions Evaders With Respect to Iran and Syria,*" (Washington, DC: The White House, May 2012), accessed November 2, 2014, http://www.gpo.gov/fdsys/pkg/FR-2012-05-03/pdf/2012-10884.pdf.

[119] Barack Obama, Executive Order 13628, *Authorizing the Implementation of Certain Sanctions Set Forth in the Iran Threat Reduction and Syria Human Rights Act of 2012 and Additional Sanctions With Respect to Iran* (Washington, DC: The White House, October 2012), accessed November 2, 2014, http://www.gpo.gov/fdsys/pkg/FR-2012-10-12/pdf/2012-25236.pdf.

[120] Jones and Ford, "U.S. Policy Toward Syria," April 11, 2013.

[121] Ibid.

[122] Ibid.

[123] Ibid.

[124] Glenn Kessler, "President Obama and the 'Red Line' on Syria's Chemical Weapons," *The Washington Post*, September 6, 2013, accessed November 2, 2014, http://www.washingtonpost.com/blogs/fact-checker/wp/2013/09/06/president-obama-and-the-red-line-on-syrias-chemical-weapons/.

[125] Ibid.

[126] Ibid.

[127] Office of the Press Secretary, "Government Assessment of the Syrian Government's Use of Chemical Weapons on August 21, 2013," (Washington, DC: The White House, August 2013), accessed November 2, 2014, http://www.whitehouse.gov/the-press-office/2013/08/30/government-assessment-syrian-government-s-use-chemical-weapons-august-21.

[128] James Corbett, "Turkey's False Flag Plan: What You're Not Being Told," The Corbett Report, April 3, 2014, accessed November 10, 2014, http://www.corbettreport.com/turkeys-false-flag-plan-what-youre-not-being-told/.

[129] Richard Lloyd and Theodore A. Postol, *Possible Implications of Faulty U.S. Technical Intelligence in the Damascus Nerve Agent Attack of August 21, 2014* (Cambridge, MA: Massachusetts Institute of Technology, January 2014), accessed November 10, 2014, https://s3.amazonaws.com/s3.documentcloud.org/documents/1006045/possible-implications-of-bad-intelligence.pdf.

[130] "MIT Study of Ghouta Chemical Attack Challenges U.S. Intelligence," RT.com, January 16, 2014, accessed November 10, 2014, http://rt.com/news/study-challenges-syria-chemical-attack-681/.

[131] Åke Sellström, *Final Report on the United Nations Mission to Investigate Allegations of the Use of Chemical Weapons in the Syrian Arab Republic*, The United Nations, December 12, 2013, 19, accessed November 2, 2014, https://unoda-web.s3.amazonaws.com/wp-content/uploads/2013/12/report.pdf. A link to the video announcing this report (as well as the actual report) can be found at http://webtv.un.org/topics-issues/global-issues/water/watch/ban-ki-moon-on-dr.-%C5ke-sellstr%F6ms-final-report-on-alleged-chemical-weapons'-incidents-in-syria2929516968001.

[132] Human Rights Council, *Report on the Independent International Commission of Inquiry on the Syrian Arab Republic*, United Nations, August 13, 2014, 19, accessed November 2, 2014, http://www.ohchr.org/EN/HRBodies/HRC/RegularSessions/Session27/Documents/A_HRC_27_60_ENG.doc.

[133] Laura Smith-Spark, "With more than 191,000 dead in Syria, U.N. Rights Chief Slams Global 'Paralysis'," CNN, August 22, 2013, accessed November 2, 2014, http://edition.cnn.com/2014/08/22/world/meast/syria-conflict/index.html?hpt=imi_c2.

[134] Barack Obama, *Address Before a Joint Session of the Congress on the State of the Union*," The American Presidency Project, January 28, 2014, accessed November 2, 2014, http://www.presidency.ucsb.edu/ws/index.php?pid=104596. Here the President defines citizenship as the right to vote and standing up for that right, standing up for the lives lost to gun violence, common purpose, participation in self government, and the obligation to serve.

[135] Ibid.

[136] Ibid.

[137] Ibid.

[138] Ibid.

[139] Ibid.

[140] Barack Obama, *The President's Weekly Address*, The American Presidency Project, September 7, 2013, accessed November 2, 2014, http://www.presidency.ucsb.edu/ws/?pid=104079.

[141] Ibid.

[142] Ibid.

[143] Barack Obama, *The President's Weekly Address*, The American Presidency Project, September 14, 2013, accessed November 2, 2014, http://www.presidency.ucsb.edu/ws/?pid=104098.

[144] White House Press Secretary, "Syrian Government's Use of Chemical Weapons,"August 2013. In this official press release, the white house policy shifted to include the credible threat of and use of chemical weapons against unarmed civilians by the Assad regime. Particularly damning is the careful attention paid to the number of children killed. Indiscriminate killing violates rules of war and this incident opened the door for potential U.S. military strikes in Syria. It is likely that strikes of any kind would do little to shape the outcome of the Syrian crisis, but would serve as a deterrent and message to future threats, the U.S. resolve to prevent the use of chemical weapons.

[145] Barack Obama, *Remarks by the President in Address to the Nation on Syria* (Washington, DC: The White House, September 2013), accessed November 2, 2014, http://www.whitehouse.gov/the-press-office/2013/09/10/remarks-president-address-nation-syria.

[146] Barack Obama, *Statement by the President on Syria* (Washington, DC: The White House, August 2013), accessed November 2, 2014, http://www.whitehouse.gov/the-press-office/2013/08/31/statement-president-syria.

[147] Andrew Dugan, "In U.S., Syria Emerges as a Top Problem, but Trails Economy,. September 5-8, 2013, Gallup poll, accessed November 2, 2014, http://www.gallup.com/poll/164348/syria-emerges-top-problem-trails-economy.aspx. Poll shows that the situation in Syria rose from 0% to 8% following the attack on August 21 and the subsequent media coverage. It is possible a significant portion of this concern is centered over U.S. actions and response to the use of chemical weapons by the Assad regime.

[148] Drew Desilver, "Americans are less Receptive to Moral Arguments," Pew Research Center, September 9, 2013, accessed November 2, 2014, http://www.pewresearch.org/fact-tank/2013/09/06/in-foreign-affairs-americans-are-less-receptive-to-moral-arguments/.

[149] Obama, *Address to the Nation on Syria*, September 10, 2013.

[150] Obama, *Weekly Address*, September 7, 2013.

[151] Ibid.

[152] Obama, *Weekly Address*, September 14, 2013.

[153] Robert S. Ford, "U.S. Policy Toward Syria, Opening Statement Before the Senate Foreign Relations Committee," U.S. Department of State, October 31, 2013, accessed November 2, 2014, http://www.state.gov/p/nea/rls/rm/216163.htm.

[154] Ibid.

[155] Ibid.

[156] George W. Bush, *Address Before a Joint Session of the Congress on the State of the Union*, The American Presidency Project, February 2, 2005, accessed November 11, 2014, http://www.presidency.ucsb.edu/ws/?pid=58746.

[157] Ibid.

[158] George W. Bush, *Address Before a Joint Session of the Congress on the State of the Union*, The American Presidency Project, January 31, 2006, accessed November 11, 2014, http://www.presidency.ucsb.edu/ws/?pid=65090.

[159] Ibid.

[160] George W. Bush, *Address Before a Joint Session of the Congress on the State of the Union*, The American Presidency Project, January 23, 2007, accessed November 11, 2014, http://www.presidency.ucsb.edu/ws/?pid=24446.

[161] George W. Bush, *National Security Strategy* (Washington, DC: The White House, 2002), accessed November 6, 2014, http://nssarchive.us/NSSR/2002.pdf, 5.

[162] Ibid., 6.

[163] Ibid.

[164] Ibid., 7.

[165] Ibid., 9.

[166] Ibid.

[167] Ibid.

[168] George W. Bush, *National Security Strategy* (Washington, DC: The White House, 2006), 12, accessed November 6, 2014, http://nssarchive.us/NSSR/2006.pdf.

[169] Ibid., 6.

[170] Ibid.

[171] Ibid., 38.

[172] Ibid.

[173] *National Security Act of 1947, Sec 503*, Lawfare Blog, accessed November 6, 2014, http://www.lawfareblog.com/wp-content/uploads/2013/05/National-Security-Act-1947-§502-503.pdf.

[174] James A. Barry, *Waging Covert Political Action* (Washington, DC: Central Intelligence Agency, 1993) accessed November 10, 2014, https://www.cia.gov/library/center-for-the-study-of-intelligence/kent-csi/vol36no3/pdf/v36i3a05p.pdf.

[175] *The Iran-Contra Report*, The American Presidency Project, November 19, 1987, accessed November 10, 2014, http://www.presidency.ucsb.edu/PS157/assignment%20files%20public/congressional%20report%20key%20sections.htm.

[176] Tim Shipman, "Bush Sanctions Black Ops Against Iran," *The Telegraph*, May 27, 2007, accessed November 10, 2014, http://www.telegraph.co.uk/news/worldnews/1552784/Bush-sanctions-black-ops-against-Iran.html.

[177] Larry Chin, "CIA-Assisted Plot to Overthrow Laos Failed," Global Research: Center for Research on Globalization, June 6, 2007, accessed November 10, 2014, http://www.globalresearch.ca/cia-assisted-plot-to-overthrow-laos-foiled/5890.

[178] John Light, "Drought Helped Spark Syria's Civil War—Is it One of Many Climate Wars to Come?" Moyers and Company, September 6, 2013, accessed November 10, 2014, http://billmoyers.com/2013/09/06/drought-helped-spark-syrias-civil-war-is-it-the-first-of-many-climate-wars-to-come/.

[179] Ibid.

[180] Ibid.

[181] William R. Polk, "Understanding Syria: From Pre-Civil War to Post-Assad," *The Atlantic*, December 10, 2013, accessed November 10, 2014, http://www.theatlantic.com/international/archive/2013/12/understanding-syria-from-pre-civil-war-to-post-assad/281989/.

[182] Ibid.

CHAPTER 5

CONCLUSIONS AND RECOMMENDATIONS

One-third of the population has fled the country or has been displaced internally. By the end of 2014, more than half of the population could be living as refugees—a situation conducive to future terrorism.[1]

— Brian Michael Jenkins

Introduction

This chapter will address the research and analysis above in order to draw logical conclusions as to the development of a policy narrative and its implications for future decision-making. In addition to these conclusions, this chapter will look at the implications for narrative use and provide a summary of the information contained in this paper.

Conclusions

At the outset, the author began this investigation with several questions in mind based on the literature review and the case study analysis in the previous chapter; the author concludes that narratives are nested in a hierarchy much like policy and strategy. Additionally, narratives are based on our understanding of the situation and as such precede policy in the policymaking process. Furthermore, new narratives will build upon pre-existing meta-narrative policy images and align with the larger narratives in the policy subsystems surrounding the policy issue. Finally, that policies not supported by the right narrative can create confusion for those attempting to understand the U.S. policy on a particular issue. This is not to say there are not unresolved issues or concerns; merely that in this case the evidence suggests these findings. There are obviously areas that warrant further inquiry.

Finally, the research presented in this paper shows that both the narratives offered by the Bush and Obama administrations are built upon the American meta-narrative and foreign policy narratives, yet the two are distinctly different. While it would be inappropriate for the author to judge one against the other, it does raise the question of how two administrations building on the same founding narratives can reach distinctly different policy issue narratives. Unfortunately more research would be required to discern the reasons why this occurred.

Implications for Narrative Use

Understanding that narratives bring context and meaning to complex and chaotic environments and that policies and strategies describe how the U.S. will achieve the end states necessary to solve those problems. Arguably, if one cannot tell a coherent story he or she does not understand the environment, problem, and solution well enough. Narratives are fundamentally critical to employing any form of power, but arguably more so in the information arena. This study highlights the importance of the narrative and its role in policymaking, but readers should understand that for narratives to be successful in driving operations, strategy, or policy, there are certain aspects that cannot be ignored. First, it is not simply that the words must match the deeds., or that actions must pass the media test, the narrative must be emotionally resonant with the audience.[2] In this respect, narratives must provide meaning and context for the target audience. For this to connection to happen, the narrative must be nested within the over-arching narratives, strategies, and policies above it.

Second, and probably more importantly, narratives must be true. While some might argue that less than true narratives can survive in policy debates, they have immediate consequences for any joint force commander. False narratives do more than create cognitive dissonance and widen the say-do gap, the might very well lead to bad decisions. Far too often, bad decisions result in mission failure or the deaths of soldiers, sailors, airmen, and marines. Furthermore, the wider the difference between what policymakers and commanders say and what they do, the more difficult it will be to achieve success.[3] When policymakers allow false narratives to exist, as might be the case with the Syrian regime's alleged use of chemical weapons, Joint Force Commanders are left to deal with the resulting problems that arise when the truth in those false narratives emerges.

Finally, not everyone develops the same narrative from the same problem. Individual understandings of the environment, the problem, and solutions are often influenced by values, attitudes, and beliefs. In developing U.S. narratives, policymakers, diplomats, and commanders assess the world as it is, as well as, the world they seek, through a lens of cultural values, attitudes, and beliefs. Because narratives are the foundation upon which both inform and influence activities are built, the narratives of our target audience then become as important as our own. Understanding the narratives of our allies, adversaries, and potential target audiences can facilitate in developing not only successful narratives, but also successful operations, strategies, and policies. This argument proposes that policymakers, commanders, and operators must truly understand the information environment they are working in. It is likely, then, that the lack of higher education in some cultures prevents the U.S. from understanding the narrative of those audiences the U.S. would seek to influence. Furthermore, it is unlikely from this research that foreign policymakers can shape or influence target audiences without understanding their own narrative. If it holds true that a policy narrative must resonate with U.S. audiences, both polity elite and public masses, then the same could be argued for those audiences the USG seeks to influence. According to Lieutenant Colonel Henderson, an instructor at the U.S. Army Command and General Staff College, the USG cannot shape the perception of the target audience, but can, and arguably should, provide context for those perceptions.[4] The efficacy of this context likely rests in the policy narrative's ability to nest within the target audiences meta-narrative.

Equally true is the difficulty in reconciling competing and disparate narratives. When two different stories are true, emotionally resonant, and equally logical, the resultant cognitive dissonance can lead to disenfranchisement or worse. As described above, two recent administrations proposed differing narratives within the same context and built upon the same policy images. In order to address this phenomenon, further research is required into the ability of the policy subsystem (or the meso-level in NPF terms) to provide consistency through periods of administration change.

Unexpected Findings

Truly, this research has offered the author a host of unexpected findings, but among those, one stands out as especially important in today's realm of statehood and war; the human domain. Regardless of the drivers of conflict, the problems described, the good and bad actors in the narrative, or the solutions proposed, this research makes abundantly clear that conflict is, and will likely always be, solidly in the human domain. As one draft version of U.S. Army Field Manual 3-13 proposed, "human populations are

107

the progenitors of conflict."[5] Therefore, any conflict is fundamentally social interaction where the interests of the parties involved are at odds with each other. As such, the ability to make sense of the conflict and provide solutions for the drivers of instability are not likely found in airstrikes or artillery barrages, though those are also likely to affect the psychology of the adversary. Meaningful change, then, will occur when those core grievances are allayed and the reasons for conflict are perceived to be addressed. It is with this unexpected finding of the research that the author concludes that successful policies, strategies, operations, or tactics, should begin with a narrative that allays these concerns built on truth and rooted in the narratives of the USG and those audiences the U.S. seeks to influence.

Recommendations

The literature review, case study, and analysis presented in this paper highlight the importance of understanding the power of narratives and their relationship with policy. In addition to the primary and secondary research questions, this researched has also uncovered several areas for further inquiry. There are three such areas the author believes to be the most critical for further research. They include (1) other case studies of policy change similar to the Syrian one presented here; (2) the efficacy of the narrative in leading strategy and operational plans and not in merely in a supporting role; and finally (3) the impacts and possible frameworks for influence that reconcile disparate audiences' meta-narratives or combat cognitive dissonance within an audience.

Other Case Studies With Significant Change in Narrative

This paper looked solely to one case study to determine the relationship between narratives and policy. While that case study was extremely beneficial because of the dramatic shift in narrative and policy, there are other case studies that could reinforce or refute the findings of this paper and bring to light undiscovered truths about this relationship. The author recommends that future research into this topic consider analysis of policy narrative change prior to, during, and post, major U.S. military operations like Operation Desert Shield/Desert Storm, Operation Enduring Freedom, and Operation Iraqi Freedom. Additionally, the analysis of policy narrative change during small wars may provide additional insight. For these, the author recommends evaluating those same time periods for Operation Urgent Fury, Just Cause, Deny Flight, Uphold Democracy, or other small wars and insurgencies.

Furthermore, several longer case studies are worthy of further inquiry. Libya offers a very long time period of policy to review. The reign of Muammar Qaddafi, the Libyan civil uprisings, and the killing of Ambassador J. Christopher Stevens, present a great case study of policy change that transcends several administrations and may provide insight into the consistency of the policy subsystem during administration change. In addition to Libya, the U.S. policy narrative on Russia offers a distinctly long case study as well. Given Russia's involvement in conflict areas such as Abkhazia, Crimea, South Ossetia, and Transnistria, the U.S. policy narrative could easily be compared and contrasted to other countries that the U.S. has alleged violated their neighbors' sovereignty.

Narrative Led Strategy and Operations

One of the most interesting insights discovered during this research is the power of leading with the right narrative. It is possible to conclude that a deeper understanding of the Afghan population's narrative and policy images influenced Gen McChrystal's significant change in transitioning from nighttime raids to daytime operations in Afghanistan in 2010. With this as a possible indications of the power of leading with the right narrative, further research could be devoted to developing an understanding of narrative led strategy and operations. Here the author argues that the current understanding of influence as shaping perceptions might not be the most successful approach.

The research above argues that narratives do not shape perception, but rather offer context and meaning. Further inquiry in this area may support or refute the claim that successful operations must take into consideration not only the U.S. narratives, but also the narratives of those audiences the U.S. seeks to influence. If this argument is true, it could fundamentally change how the U.S. develops strategies and plans, as well as significantly change the current U.S. inform and influence doctrine.

Cognitive Dissonance and Competing Narratives

The last major area for further inquiry is in understanding the impacts of competing narratives. This further research could provide insight on how dominant policy images or narratives emerge. The research above suggests that it is possible to have multiple narratives, both of which are supported by and nested with those narratives in the hierarchy above it, that are seemingly at odds with each other. This competition for dominance could bring to light the effects of cognitive dissonance. Here further research is needed to understand how the U.S. can provide a narrative that is both aligned to the U.S. meta-narrative but also rooted in the policy images and narrative of those audiences the U.S. seeks to influence.

Additionally, this research has proposed that battlefield commanders must deal with the immediate consequences of a false or less than true narrative. It is equally possible that the cognitive dissonance that arises from these false narratives when contrasted with operational experience could result in some manifestation of post-traumatic stress disorder. Here further research is required to understand how individuals reconcile these competing narratives and make sense of their understanding of the world.

Summary and Conclusions

This research has found that a consistent narrative and corresponding policy are integral to successful political action. Inconsistencies between the two can erode both public and elite confidences in the policymaker's ability to successful pursue appropriate policy end states. In much the same way that policies and strategy are interwoven through a nested hierarchy of precedence, so too are the narratives about those policies and strategies. By understanding this relationship policymaker's can more effectively articulate their understanding of the policy issue and their recommended solutions. Successful narratives build upon the simpler policy images of the higher echelon narratives while still describing complex issues in simple, emotionally resonant, and supportable messages. This strategic communication is essential to competing in an embattled discourse arena where the multitude of voices contributes to the cacophony of narratives. War is the human domain, "delivering the message of war requires appropriate deeds as well as the right words."[6]

111

However, it is not just the U.S. foreign policy narratives that will help shape the attitudes and beliefs of the citizens of potential conflict areas found in failing and fragile states, the U.S. must also seek to enable the leadership and narratives of the moderate segments of those populations as they struggle for policy reform. In this respect, the U.S. can learn from the advice of T.E. Lawrence, who said, "Do not try to do too much with your own hands. Better the Arabs do it tolerably, than that you do it perfectly. It is their war, and you are to help them, not win it for them."[7]

Finally, narratives, such as those addressed in this case study, articulate priorities and agendas resulting in the means available for addressing an international policy arena fraught with peril, especially when considering the introduction of military force. This research suggests that operations led by consistent narratives and informed by the culture and people of the region will likely have better success than those which are based solely on military objectives that lack the deeper connection to a grander strategy and policy.

---

[1] Jenkins, *The Dynamics of Syria's Civil War*. In his research article for the RAND Corporation, Jenkins's research suggests that the Syrian crisis of displaced persons could reach half the population by the end of 2014. He further asserts that refugee camps could serve as a breeding ground for future terrorism.

[2] A colloquial phrase where if one assesses the potential action to reflect negatively on the command, service, military, or nation if that action were on the front page of a newspaper, or breaking news on some media of press.

[3] Eric D. Henderson, conversation with the author, November 14, 2014. LTC Henderson is an instructor in the Department of Joint, Interagency, and Multinational Operations at the U.S. Army Command and General Staff College with extensive experience in Information Operations as an Army Functional Area 30 Branch Officer.

[4] Ibid.

[5] U.S. Department of the Army, Field Manual 3-13, *Inform and Influence Activities – Draft Version*, n.d. This document was given to the author by Lieutenant

Colonel Eric Henderson, an instructor at the U.S. Army Command and General Staff College.

[6] David and McKeldin, *Ideas as Weapons,* xii.

[7] T. E. Lawrence, "Twenty-Seven Articles," *The Arab Bulletin*, August 20, 1917.

BIBLIOGRAPHY

Books

David, G. J. Jr., and T. R. McKeldin III, eds. *Ideas as Weapons: Influence and Perception in Modern Warfare*. Dulles, VA: Potomac Books, 2009.

Erlich, Reese W. *Conversations with Terrorists: Middle East Leaders on Politics, Violence, and Empire*. San Francisco: PoliPointPress, 2010.

Hubbard, Elbert. *The Moto Book*. East Aurora, NY: Roycroft Press, 1907.

Kubiak, Jeffrey J. *War Narratives and the American National Will in War*. New York, NY: Palgrave-Macmillan, 2014.

Nin, Anais. *Seduction of the Minotaur*. Chicago, IL: Swallow Press, 1961.

True, James L., Bruan D. Jones, and Frank R. Baumgartner. "Punctuated-Equilibrium Theory: Explaining Stability and Change in Public Policymaking." In *Theories of the Policy Process*, edited by Paul A. Sabatier, 155-187. Boulder, CO: Westview, 2007.

Waller, J. Michael. *Fighting the War of Ideas Like a Real War*. Washington, DC: The Institute of World Politics, 2007.

Periodicals

Benford, Robert D., and David A. Snow. "Framing Processes and Social Movements: An Overview and Assessment." *Annual Review of Sociology* 26 (2000): 611-639.

Burkeman, Oliver. "Obama Administration Says Goodbye to 'War on Terror'." *The Guardian*. March 25, 2009. Accessed November 2, 2014. http://www.theguardian .com/world/2009/mar/25/obama-war-terror-overseas-contingency-operations

Jakes, Lara, and Rebecca Santana. "Iraq Withdrawal: U.S. Abandoning Plans To Keep Troops in Country." *The Huffington Post*. October 25, 2011. Accessed November 2, 2014. http://www.huffingtonpost.com/2011/10/15/iraq-withdrawal-us-troops_n _1012661.html

Herrmann, Richard K., James F. Voss, Tonya Y.E. Schooler, and Joseph Ciarrochi. "Images in International Relations: An Experimental Test of Cognitive Schemata." *International Studies Quarterly* 41, no. 3 (September 1997): 403-433.

Lawrence, T.E., "Twenty-Seven Articles." *The Arab Bulletin* (August 20, 1917).

Rose, Gideon. "Neoclassical Realism and Theories of Foreign Policy." *World Politics* 51, no. 1 (October, 1998): 144-172.

Shanahan, Elizabeth A., Michael D. Jones, and Mark K. McBeth. "Policy Narratives and Policy Processes." *Policy Studies Journal* 39, no. 3 (2011): 535-561.

Shanahan, Mike. "What's in a narrative? In Policy, Everything or Nothing." *International Institute for Environment and Development.* September 28, 2012. Accessed September 17, 2014. http://www.iied.org/what-s-narrative-policy-everything-or-nothing.

Steinberg, Marc W. "Tilting the Frame: Considerations on Collective Action Framing from a Discursive Turn." *Theory and Society* 27, no. 6 (December 1998): 845-872.

Government Documents

Barry, James A. *Waging Covert Political Action.* Washington DC: Central Intelligence Agency, 1993. Accessed November 10, 2014. https://www.cia.gov/ library/center-for-the-study-of-intelligence/kent-csi/vol36no3/pdf/v36i3a05p.pdf.

Bureau of Near Eastern Affairs. "U.S. Relations With Syria Fact Sheet." U.S. Department of State. March 20, 2014. Accessed November 2, 2014. http://www.state.gov/r/pa/ ei/bgn/3580.htm.

Burns, William J. "Remarks on Middle East Peace Following Meeting with Syrian President Bashar al-Assad." U.S. Department of State. February 17, 2010. Accessed November 2, 2014. http://www.state.gov/p/us/rm/2010/136717.htm.

Bush, George H. W. *Address to the Nation on the Situation in Somalia.* The American Presidency Project, December 4, 1992. Accessed October 31, 2014. http://www. presidency.ucsb.edu/ws/?pid=21758.

Bush, George W. *Address Before a Joint Session of the Congress on the United States Response to the Terrorist Attacks of September 11.* The American Presidency Project. September 20, 2001. Accessed October 31, 2014, http://www.presidency. ucsb.edu/ws/?pid=64731.

———. *Address Before a Joint Session of the Congress on the State of the Union.* The American Presidency Project. February 2, 2005. Accessed November 11, 2014. http://www.presidency.ucsb.edu/ws/?pid=58746.

———. *Address Before a Joint Session of the Congress on the State of the Union.* The American Presidency Project, January 31, 2006. Accessed November 11, 2014. http://www.presidency.ucsb.edu/ws/?pid=65090.

———. *Address Before a Joint Session of the Congress on the State of the Union.* The American Presidency Project. January 23, 2007. Accessed November 11, 2014. http://www.presidency.ucsb.edu/ws/?pid=24446.

———. Executive Order 13441, *Blocking Property of Persons Undermining the Sovereignty of Lebanon or Its Democratic Processes and Institutions*. The American Presidency Project. August 1, 2007. Accessed November 2, 2014. http://www.presidency.ucsb.edu/ws/?pid=75641.

———. *National Security Strategy*. Washington, DC: The White House, 2002. Accessed November 6, 2014. http://nssarchive.us/NSSR/2002.pdf.

———. *National Security Strategy*. Washington, DC: The White House, 2006. Accessed November 6, 2014. http://nssarchive.us/NSSR/2006.pdf.

Central Intelligence Agency. "Syria." The World Factbook. Accessed August 13, 2014. https://www.cia.gov/library/publications/the-world-factbook/geos/sy.html.

Chairman, Joint Chiefs of Staff. *National Military Strategy*. Washington, DC: Joint Chiefs of Staff, 2010.

Clinton, Hillary R. "Recent Events in Tunisia in a Press Statement." U.S. Department of State. January 14, 2011. Accessed November 2, 2014. http://www.state.gov/secretary/20092013clinton/rm/2011/01/154684.htm.

———. "Remarks at Press Availability." U.S. Department of State. April 15, 2011. Accessed November 2, 2014. http://www.state.gov/secretary/20092013clinton/rm/2011/04/160998.htm.

——— "Remarks on Libya and Syria." U.S. Department of State. July 15, 2011. Accessed November 6, 2014. http://www.state.gov/secretary/20092013clinton/rm/2011/07/168656.htm.

———. "Secretary Clinton Supports Syrian People in Op-Ed." U.S. Department of State. June 17, 2011. Accessed November 4, 2014. http://www.state.gov/r/pa/prs/ps/2011/06/166488.htm.

———. "Syrian Convictions of Human Rights Activists Press Conference." U.S. Department of State. July 5, 2010. Accessed November 2, 2014. http://www.state.gov/secretary/20092013clinton/rm/2010/07/143966.htm.

———. "Violence in Yemen in a Press Statement." U.S. State Department. March 18, 2011. Accessed November 2, 2014. http://www.state.gov/secretary/20092013clinton/rm/2011/03/158597.htm.

Clinton, William J. "Letter to Congressional Leaders on the Situation in Somalia." The American Presidency Project. June 10, 1993. Accessed October 31, 2014. http://www.presidency.ucsb.edu/ws/?pid=46676.

Crowley, Philip J. "Protests in Algeria in a Press Statement." U.S. Department of State. February 13, 2011. Accessed November 2, 2014. http://www.state.gov/r/pa/prs/ps/2011/02/156515.htm.

———. "Situation in Algeria in a Press Statement." U.S. Department of State. February 20, 2011. Accessed November 2, 2014. http://www.state.gov/r/pa/prs/ps/2011/02/156829.htm.

———. "Situation in Egypt in a Press Statement." U.S. Department of State. January 25, 2011. Accessed November 2, 2014. http://www.state.gov/r/pa/prs/ps/2011/01/155307.htm.

———. "Situation in Lebanon in a Press Statement." U.S. Department of State. January 25, 2011. Accessed November 2, 2014. http://www.state.gov/r/pa/prs/ps/2011/01/155303.htm

Feltman, Jeffrey D. "Acting Assistant Secretary Feltonman Briefs on Meetings with Syrian Officials." U.S. Department of State. March 7, 2009. Accessed November 2, 2014, http://www.state.gov/r/pa/prs/ps/2009/03/120122.htm.

———. "U.S.-Syria Relations Press Conference." U.S. Department of State. March 6, 2009. Accessed November 2, 2014. http://www.state.gov/p/ nea/rls/rm/2009/120084.htm.

Ford, Robert S. "U.S. Policy Toward Syria, Opening Statement Before the Senate Foreign Relations Committee." U.S. Department of State. October 31, 2013. Accessed November 2, 2014. http://www.state.gov/p/nea/rls/rm/216163.htm.

Jones, Elizabeth, and Robert S. Ford. "U.S. Policy Toward Syria, Senate Foreign Relations Committee." U.S. Department of State. April 11, 2013. Accessed November 2, 2014. http://www.state.gov/p/nea/rls/rm/2013/207416.htm.

National Security Act of 1947, Sec 503. Lawfare Blog. Accessed November 6, 2014. http://www.lawfareblog.com/wp-content/uploads/2013/05/National-Security-Act-1947-§502-503.pdf.

Nuland, Victoria. "U.S. Condemns Ongoing Violence in Syria." U.S. Department of State. July 25, 2011. Accessed November 6, 2014. http://www.state.gov/r/pa/prs/ps/ 2011/07/169069.htm.

Obama, Barack. *Address Before a Joint Session of the Congress on the State of the Union.* The American Presidency Project. February 24, 2009. Accessed November 2, 2014. http://www.presidency.ucsb.edu/ws/index.php?pid=85753.

———. *Address Before a Joint Session of the Congress on the State of the Union.* The American Presidency Project. January 27, 2010. Accessed October 30, 2014. http://www.presidency.ucsb.edu/ws/index.php?pid=87433.

———. *Address Before a Joint Session of the Congress on the State of the Union.* The American Presidency Project. January 25, 2011. Accessed October 30, 2014. http://www.presidency.ucsb.edu/ws/index.php?pid=88928.

———. *Address Before a Joint Session of the Congress on the State of the Union.* The American Presidency Project. January 24, 2012. Accessed November 2, 2014. http://www.presidency.ucsb.edu/ws/index.php?pid=99000.

———. *Address Before a Joint Session of the Congress on the State of the Union.* The American Presidency Project. February 12, 2013. Accessed November 2, 2014. http://www.presidency.ucsb.edu/ws/index.php?pid=102826.

———. *Address Before a Joint Session of the Congress on the State of the Union.* The American Presidency Project. January 28, 2014. Accessed November 2, 2014. http://www.presidency.ucsb.edu/ws/index.php?pid=104596.

———. Executive Order 13572, *Blocking Property of Certain Persons With Respect to Human Rights Abuses in Syria.* Washington, DC: The White House, April 2011. Accessed November 2, 2014. http://www.gpo.gov/fdsys/pkg/FR-2011-05-03/pdf/ 2011-10910.pdf.

———. Executive Order 13573, *Blocking Property of Senior Officials of the Government of Syria.* Washington, DC: The White House, May 2011. Accessed November 2, 2014. http://www.gpo.gov/ fdsys/pkg/FR-2011-05-20/pdf/2011-12645.pdf.

———. Executive Order 13582, *Blocking Property of the Government of Syria and Prohibiting Certain Transactions With Respect to Syria.* Washington, DC: The White House August 2011. Accessed November 2, 2014. http://www.gpo.gov/ fdsys/pkg/FR-2011-08-22/pdf/2011-21505.pdf.

———. Executive Order 13606, *Blocking Property and Suspending Entry Into the United States of Certain Persons With Respect to Grave Human Rights abuses by the Governments of Iran and Syria via Information Technology.* Washington DC: The White House, April 2012. Accessed November 2, 2014. http://www.gpo.gov/fdsys/pkg/FR-2012-04-24/pdf/2012-10034.pdf.

———. Executive Order 13608, *Prohibiting Certain Transactions With and Suspending Entry Into the United States of Foreign Sanctions Evaders With Respect to Iran and Syria.* Washington, DC: The White House, May 2012. Accessed November 2, 2014. http://www.gpo.gov/fdsys/pkg/FR-2012-05-03/pdf/2012-10884.pdf.

———. Executive Order 13628, *Authorizing the Implementation of Certain Sanctions Set Forth in the Iran Threat Reduction and Syria Human Rights Act of 2012 and Additional Sanctions With Respect to Iran.* Washington, DC: The White House, October 2012. Accessed November 2, 2014. http://www.gpo.gov/fdsys/pkg/FR-2012-10-12/pdf/2012-25236.pdf.

———. *Message to the Congress on Continuation of the National Emergency With Respect to the Actions of the Government of Syria*. The American Presidency Project. May 3, 2010. Accessed November 2, 2014. http://www.presidency.ucsb.edu/ws/?pid=87896.

———. *National Security Strategy*. Washington, DC: The White House, 2010.

———. *Notice on Continuation of the National Emergency With Respect to the Actions of the Government of Syria*. The American Presidency Project. May 7, 2009. Accessed November 2, 2014. http://www.presidency.ucsb.edu/ws/ ?pid=86115.

———. *Notice on Continuation of the National Emergency With Respect to the Actions of Certain Persons To Undermine the Sovereignty of Lebanon or Its Democratic Processes and Institutions*. The American Presidency Project. July 30, 2009. Accessed November 2, 2014, http://www.presidency.ucsb.edu/ws/ ?pid=86480.

———. *Notice: Continuation of the National Emergency With Respect to the Actions of Certain Persons To Undermine the Sovereignty of Lebanon or Its Democratic Processes and Institutions*. The American Presidency Project. July 29, 2010. Accessed November 2, 2014. http://www.presidency.ucsb.edu/ws/ ?pid=88257.

———. *Remarks by the President in Address to the Nation on Syria*. Washington, DC: The White House, September 2013. Accessed May 1, 2014. http://www. whitehouse.gov/the-press-office/2013/09/10/remarks-president-address-nation-syria.

———. *Statement by the President on Syria*. Washington, DC: The White House, August 2013. Accessed November 2, 2014. http://www.whitehouse.gov/the-press-office/ 2013/08/31/statement-president-syria.

———. *The President's Weekly Address*. The American Presidency Project. September 7, 2013. Accessed November 2, 2014. http://www.presidency.ucsb.edu/ws/?pid= 104079.

———. *The President's Weekly Address*. The American Presidency Project. September 10, 2011. Accessed November 2, 2014. http://www.presidency.ucsb.edu/ws/?pid= 96668.

———. *The President's Weekly Address*. The American Presidency Project. September 14, 2013. Accessed November 2, 2014. http://www.presidency.ucsb.edu/ws/?pid= 104098.

———. *The President's Weekly Address*. The American Presidency Project. September 26, 2009. Accessed October 17, 2014. http://www.presidency.ucsb.edu/ws/?pid= 86683.

Office of the Press Secretary. *Government Assessment of the Syrian Government's Use of Chemical Weapons on August 21, 2013*. Washington, DC: The White House. August 2013. Accessed November 2, 2014. http://www.whitehouse.gov/the-press-office/2013/ 08/30/government-assessment-syrian-government-s-use-chemical-weapons-august-21.

Sharp, Jeremy M. *Syria: Issues for the 112th Congress and Background on U.S. Sanctions.* Washington, DC: Congressional Research Service, 2011.

Sullivan, Jake. "Briefing on Recent Developments in the Middle East and Other Issues." U.S. Department of State. April 26, 2011. Accessed November 2, 2014. http:// www.state.gov/p/nea/rls/rm/161818.htm.

The Iran-Contra Report. The American Presidency Project. November 19, 1987. Accessed November 10, 2014. http://www.presidency.ucsb.edu/PS157/ assignment%20files%20public/congressional%20report%20key%20sections.htm.

Toner, Mark C. "Violence in Syria." U.S. Department of State. March 23, 2011. Accessed November 2, 2014. http://www.state.gov/r/pa/prs/ps/2011/03/ 158894.htm.

U.S. Congress. *Syria Accountability and Lebanese Sovereignty Act of 2003*. H. Res. 1828, 108th Cong., December 12, 2003. Accessed October 14, 2014. https://www. govtrack.us/congress/ bills/108/hr1828/text.

U.S. Department of the Army. Field Manual 3-24.2, *Tactics in Counterinsurgency*. Washington, DC: U.S. Department of the Army, April 2009.

———. Army Doctrine Publication 5-0, *The Operations Process*. Washington DC: U.S. Department of the Army, May 2012.

———, Field Manual 3-13, *Inform and Influence Activities – Draft Version*. Washington, DC: U.S. Department of the Army, no date.

U.S. Department of State. "Background Briefing by Senior Administration Officials on Syria." June 17, 2011. Accessed November 4, 2014. http://www.state.gov/p/nea /rls/rm/166484.htm.

———. "U.S. Relations with Syria." March 20, 2014. Accessed October 14, 2014. http://www.state.gov/r/pa/ei/bgn/3580.htm.

U.S. Department of the Treasury. "Syria Sanctions Program." August 2, 2013. Accessed October 7, 2014. http://www.treasury.gov/resource-center/sanctions/Programs/ Documents/syria.pdf.

U.S. Joint Chiefs of Staff. Joint Publication 1-02, *Department of Defense Dictionary of Military and Associated Terms*. Washington, DC: U.S. Joint Chiefs of Staff, November 2010.

————. Joint Publication 3-24, *Counterinsurgency*. Washington, DC: Joint Chiefs of Staff, 2013.

————. Joint Publication 3-13, *Information Operations*. Washington, DC: U.S. Joint Chiefs of Staff, November 2012.

Other Sources

Associated Press. "Syrian Uprising Timeline of Key Events." September 4, 2013. Accessed November 2, 2014. http://www.politico.com/story/2013/09/syria-timeline-96270.html.

Chin, Larry. "CIA-Assisted Plot to Overthrow Laos Failed." Global Research: Center for Research on Globalization. June 6, 2007. Accessed November 10, 2014. http://www.globalresearch.ca/cia-assisted-plot-to-overthrow-laos-foiled/5890.

CNN Wire Staff. "CNN Fact Check: A day after Libya attack, Obama described it as 'acts of terror'." CNN Politics. October 17, 2012. Accessed November 2, 2014. http://www.cnn.com/2012/10/17/politics/fact-check-terror/index.html.

Corbett, James. "Turkey's False Flag Plan: What You're Not Being Told." The Corbett Report. April 3, 2014. Accessed November 10, 2014. http://www.corbettreport.com/turkeys-false-flag-plan-what-youre-not-being-told/.

Daragahi, Borzou, and Alexandra Sandels. "Syrian Troops Fire on Protesters, 34 Killed." *Los Angeles Times*. May 20, 2011. Accessed November 2, 2014. http://articles.latimes.com/2011/may/20/world/la-fg-syria-protests-kurds-20110521.

Desilver, Drew. "Americans are less Receptive to Moral Arguments." Pew Research Center. Accessed November 2, 2014. http://www.pewresearch.org/fact-tank/2013/09/06/in-foreign-affairs-americans-are-less-receptive-to-moral-arguments/

Deutschman, Alan. "Change or Die." Fast Company. May 2005. Accessed August 11, 2014. http://www.fastcompany.com/52717/change-or-die.

Dugan, Andrew. "In U.S., Syria Emerges as a Top Problem, but Trails Economy." Gallup Poll. September 8, 2013. Accessed November 2, 2014, http://www.gallup.com/poll/164348/syria-emerges-top-problem-trails-economy.aspx.

Freedom House. *Freedom in the World*. 2014. Accessed October 7, 2014. http://www.freedomhouse.org.

————. "Syria." *Freedom in the World*, 2013.accessed August 13, 2014, http://www.freedomhouse.org/report/freedom-world/2014/syria-0#.U_agp0uQYYU.

Goodennough, Patrick. "Syrian President Assad Regarded as a 'Reformer,' Clinton Says." CBS News. March 28, 2011. Accessed October 7, 2014. http://cnsnews.com/news/article/syrian-president-assad-regarded-reformer-clinton-says.

Heritage Foundation. "Syria." *The 2014 Index of Economic Freedom*. Accessed August 28, 2014. http://www.heritage.org/index/country/syria.

Human Rights Council. "Report on the Independent International Commission of Inquiry on the Syrian Arab Republic." United Nations. 2014. Accessed August 13, 2014. http://www.ohchr.org/EN/HRBodies/HRC/RegularSessions/Session27/Documents/A_HRC_27_60_ENG.doc.

Human Rights Watch. "Syria: President Assad Fails to Deliver Reform." March 30, 2011. Accessed October 7, 2014. http://www.hrw.org/news/2011/03/30/syria-president-asad-fails-deliver-reform.

Internet Encyclopedia of Philosophy. "Bakhtin Circle." Accessed October 27, 2014. http://www.iep.utm.edu/bakhtin/.

Jenkins, Brian Michael. *The Dynamics of Syria's Civil War*. Santa Monica, CA: RAND Corporation, 2014. Accessed April 28, 2014. http://www.rand.org/pubs/perspectives/PE115.html.

Kessler, Glenn. "President Obama and the 'Red Line' on Syria's Chemical Weapons." *The Washington Post*. September 6, 2013. Accessed November 2, 2014. http://www.washingtonpost.com/blogs/fact-checker/wp/2013/09/06/president-obama-and-the-red-line-on-syrias-chemical-weapons/.

Light, John. "Drought Helped Spark Syria's Civil War—Is it One of Many Climate Wars to Come?" Moyers ad Company. September 6, 2013. Accessed November 10, 2014. http://billmoyers.com/2013/09/06/drought-helped-spark-syrias-civil-war-is-it-the-first-of-many-climate-wars-to-come/.

Lynch, Marc. "Obama's Arab Spring?" *Foreign Policy*. January 6, 2011. Accessed August 13, 2014. http://mideastafrica.foreignpolicy.com/posts/2011/01/06/obamas_arab_spring.

Polk, William R. "Understanding Syria: From Pre-Civil War to Post-Assad." *The Atlantic*. December 10, 2013. Accessed November 10, 2014. http://www.theatlantic.com/international/archive/2013/12/understanding-syria-from-pre-civil-war-to-post-assad/281989/.

RT.com. "MIT Study of Ghouta Chemical Attack Challenges U.S. Intelligence." January 16, 2014. Accessed November 10, 2014. http://rt.com/news/study-challenges-syria-chemical-attack-681/.

Sellström, Åke. *Final Report on the United Nations Mission to Investigate Allegations of the Use of Chemical Weapons in the Syrian Arab Republic.* The United Nations. December 12, 2013. Accessed November 2, 2014. https://unoda-web.s3. amazonaws.com/ wp-content/uploads/2013/12/report.pdf.

Shipman, Tim. "Bush Sanctions Black Ops Against Iran." The Telegraph. May 27, 2007. Accessed November 10, 2014. http://www.telegraph.co.uk/news/worldnews/ 1552784/Bush-sanctions-black-ops-against-Iran.html.

Smith-Spark, Laura. "With more than 191,000 dead in Syria, U.N. Rights Chief Slams Global 'Paralysis'." CNN. August 22, 2013. Accessed November 2, 2014. http://edition.cnn.com/2014/08/22/world/meast/syria-conflict/index.html ?hpt=imi_c2.

Richard, Lloyd, and Theodore A. Postol. *Possible Implications of Faulty U.S. Technical Intelligence in the Damascus Nerve Agent Attack of August 21, 2014.* Cambridge, MA: Massachusetts Institute of Technology, January 2014. Accessed November 10, 2014, https://s3.amazonaws.com/s3.documentcloud.org/documents/1006045/ possible-implications-of-bad-intelligence.pdf.

Syrian Martyrs. "Martyr Counts by Month." Accessed November 2, 2014. http://syrianshuhada.com/default.asp?lang=en&a=st&st=8.

Vuechner Institute for Governance, University of Colorado at Denver. "Advocacy Coalition Framework." UC Denver Online. Accessed October 14, 2014. http://www.ucdenver.edu/academics/colleges/SPA/BuechnerInstitute/Centers/WO PPR/ACF/Pages/ACFOverview.aspx.

World Tribune. "Defecting troops from 'Free Syrian Army', target Assad Security Forces." August 3, 2011. Accessed November 2, 2014. http://www.worldtribune. com/worldtribune/WTARC/2011/me_syria0973_08_03.asp.

Yarger, Harry R. "Strategic Theory for the 21st Century: The Little Book on Big Strategy." Monograph, Strategic Studies Institute, February 2006. Accessed October 7, 2014. http://www.strategicstudiesinstitute.army.mil/pubs/download. cfm?q=641.